OTHELLO

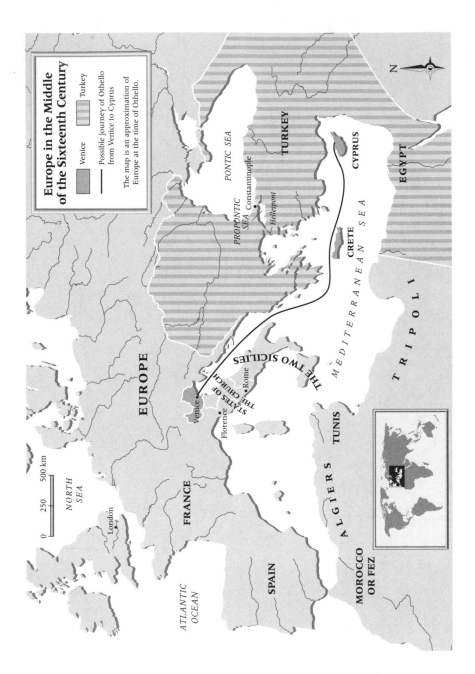

Europe in the Middle
of the Sixteenth Century

Venice

Turkey

Possible journey of Othello
from Venice to Cyprus

The map is an approximation of
Europe at the time of Othello.

N

EUROPE

ATLANTIC
OCEAN

NORTH
SEA

London

FRANCE

SPAIN

MOROCCO
OR FEZ

ALGIERS

TUNIS

Venice

Florence

STATES OF
THE CHURCH

Rome

THE TWO SICILIES

MEDITERRANEAN SEA

TRIPOLI

CRETE

CYPRUS

EGYPT

PONTIC SEA

PROPONTIC
SEA

Constantinople

Hellespont

TURKEY

0   250   500 km

HARCOURT SHAKESPEARE

OTHELLO

Series Editor: Ken Roy

edited by Ken Roy

NELSON EDUCATION

The illustrations in Harcourt Shakespeare's *Othello* depict some of the variations in clothing style of the period in which the play is set as well as the period in which *Othello* was first performed.

Canadian Cataloguing in Publication Data
Shakespeare, William, 1564–1616
   Othello

(Harcourt Shakespeare)
1st ed.
ISBN-13 : 978-0-7747-1478-5
ISBN-10 : 0-7747-1478-6

1. Shakespeare, William, 1564–1616. Othello. I. Roy, Ken. II. Title. III. Series

PR2829.A2R69 2000   822.3'3   C00-932761-4

Harcourt Shakespeare: Series Editor, Ken Roy

Project Manager: Deborah Davidson
Developmental Editor: Jane Clark
Editor: Brett Savory
Senior Production Editors: Sharon Dzubinsky, Karin Fediw
Copy Editor: Susan McNish
Production Coordinator: Cheri Westra
Page Composition: Christine Gambin, Carolyn Hutchings Sebestyen
Cover and Text Illustrations: Henry Van Der Linde

Printed in Canada
8 9 10 11   14 13 12 11

To the Reader

Othello is a strange play. It strikes many people as a cynical commentary on humanity and the depths to which it can sink, but it also suggests that humanity can rise above the negativism that pervades on all sides. Others see the play as an epic poem about love. Whatever the perspective, the play gives incredible insight into how we all function as human beings because it raises questions that we simply cannot answer. What makes us all function is often, indeed, a great mystery.

The story is not a new one: Othello is a fine man of impeccable military background who simply falls in love. When he does, he lets go of his military judgement and unleashes his emotions. Falling in love can be dangerous, as he discovers. The play differs from other Shakespearean tragedies in that it has no subplot: it focuses entirely on Othello. As a result, the play has an intensity that is unique.

As you read, you will encounter motivations of love, hate, pride, revenge, vindictiveness, vulnerability, and what you might regard as outright evil. These issues might remind you of situations you have seen on TV and encountered in real life. You will probably find that the issues and questions raised in the play are the same ones that Shakespeare's audiences had to deal with.

To some people, *Othello* is a fairy tale gone wrong. To others, it is a play about the conflict of good and evil. Whatever stance you take, you will find yourself engaged with the characters and their predicaments.

Before each scene are some questions and suggestions that will help you explore the play's ideas and themes. Your personal responses to these will contribute to your understanding of the play's impact and intent.

The activities encourage you to discuss and make decisions cooperatively in groups and to share your findings with the class as a whole. As well, you will write personal responses to the play in your own journal.

Each scene is followed by activities related specifically to it. You may choose to respond to each scene as you finish reading it, or you may prefer to wait until an entire act has evolved

1

before you respond. Most of the activities, like the questions preceding each scene, invite both group and personal responses.

Now that you have some idea of what the play is about and of the various ways you can experience it, you are ready to begin your own personal encounter with an exciting and rewarding experience.

Getting Started

Everyone knows stories in which things don't turn out the way they are supposed to. Fairy tales provide us with many points of reference, although they usually conclude with a happy ending. Love is a powerful theme in this type of story, and we all relate to such tales because we all hope that love will ultimately triumph. Sometimes it doesn't. Fairy tales rarely depict what life is about, but often they can be a starting point toward understanding a play as complex as *Othello*.

The following activities will help you explore some of the issues that you will encounter in reading the play. Keep an open mind, and be willing to refine and even change your opinions as you go along. Your own opinions and reactions make great journal entries and can help you determine your own progress as you think the play through.

Let's begin with a fairy tale ...

1. Read "Beauty and the Beast." As you will discover, this is a story about a young woman who finds true love in a most peculiar way. With your group or privately in your journal, respond to the following:

    *   While "Beauty and the Beast" has a happy ending, what could have happened to turn the story the other way?
    *   Can a person ever really become a "beast," at least in terms of behaviour? Make a list of the qualities that, in your opinion, constitute "beastly" behaviour.
    *   Where do we get our notions about beasts, anyway? What do beasts symbolize for us? Make a list of some current human "beasts" that come to mind. Where and when did these people step over the line?

2

- Is it possible to transform a "beast"? What redeems the beast in the fairy tale?

  Write your own version of this fairy tale so that the ending isn't a happy one. How does the ending you wrote differ from the original one? How does it affect the whole story? How does this awareness help you to distinguish tragedy from comedy? How would you define these two genres? What would make anyone choose to operate from a base of hatred rather than one of love? Can such people be "cured"?

2. Can a person buy love? Make a personal journal entry in response to this question.

3. You probably know somebody who never agrees with anyone else's decisions. Discuss what you think makes such people behave as they do. How do you deal with them? In your journal, write an advice article that might help such individuals relate to others more successfully.

4. Some people thrive by manipulating others. Describe such a person. What do you think motivates such people? Do they usually succeed, or do people eventually recognize them for what they are? Record a personal experience involving such a person, and explain how you felt about it.

5. Have you ever wanted to change the ending of a story or a movie? Think of one, and describe what changes you would have made. Which ending do you think *really* works—yours or the original one?

6. Write an extensive journal response on your perception of issues related to the following: belonging, power, privilege, and identity. Consider questions such as the following:

   - How important to most people is security about their "place" or social status?
   - How can focusing on any one of the above issues change a person's life?
   - How do any of these concepts influence what goes on in our own society?
   - How important is it for people to "know who they are"?
   - Why do you think people pay attention to any of the above concepts at all?

3

7. With your group, discuss what you think the roles of husbands and wives should be in relation to each other. From your current observations of our society, are your criteria usually met? If so, explain how. If not, what do you think should be done? If change is needed, who is best qualified to initiate it— the husband or the wife?

8. We have all experienced times when we have been insulted, discounted, and excluded. In your journal, recall an incident in which one of these things happened to you. How did you deal with the situation? Did it change the way you dealt with people thereafter?

9. Look up the word "narcissism" and read the myth of Narcissus. How can a character trait like narcissism destroy a person? In your opinion, what causes narcissistic tendencies in certain people? Write a journal entry about narcissism as social insecurity, and recount an incident that you consider applicable to prove your point.

10. Discuss with your group what is so fascinating about holding power. Do you believe people with power are more attractive than those without it? In your journal, describe an occasion when you wanted some form of power. What did you do and what was the outcome?

There are, of course, many other ways to approach the play. One way is to look up the sources of *Othello* and the character on whom the play is based. This might help you to make some predictions about what Shakespeare did with the story. As you read the play, you can make notes about what Shakespeare did with the original source and decide how you might have treated the story had you been writing a play about it.

These suggestions are intended to get you thinking about some of the issues you will encounter in your reading of the play. Whatever you choose to do, the activities at the end of each scene and act will provide you with many more opportunities to interact with this play. Choose the ones you find most interesting, and, in doing them, you will find that your deepened involvement with the text enables you to broaden your horizons and increase your awareness of how literature can enhance experience.

Dramatis Personae

(Characters in the Play)

Duke of Venice
Brabantio, a Senator
Other Senators
Gratiano, brother to Brabantio
Lodovico, kinsman to Brabantio
Othello, a noble Moor in the service of the Venetian state
Cassio, his lieutenant
Iago, his ancient
Roderigo, a Venetian gentleman
Montano, Othello's predecessor in the government of Cyprus
Clown, servant to Othello
Desdemona, daughter to Brabantio and wife to Othello
Emilia, wife to Iago
Bianca, mistress to Cassio
Sailor, Messenger, Herald, Officers, Gentlemen, Musicians, and
    Attendants

Scene: Venice, and a seaport in Cyprus

Act 1, Scene 1

In this scene ...

On a street in Venice, Iago is in conversation with Roderigo, a young Venetian, who is upset because his courtship of Brabantio's daughter Desdemona has failed, and she has eloped with the moor Othello. Roderigo blames Iago for his failure to help him in his courtship despite the money he has paid for that help. Iago assures him that he, too, hates Othello because the important military position of lieutenant has gone to Cassio (who is from Florence) and Iago has been given instead the lesser position of ensign (ancient) or personal attendant. Iago argues that he did not know of the couple's plans for the elopement and convinces Roderigo that he should inform Desdemona's father of what his daughter has done. Iago accompanies Roderigo to Brabantio's house where Roderigo announces the news. Enraged, Brabantio demands that Roderigo lead him in an armed search for the newlyweds.

1	*Tush:* a slang expression indicating impatience; roughly, "nonsense"
2	*had:* that is, had the use of
3	*this:* referring to the elopement of Othello and Desdemona. Roderigo has been paying Iago in advance to help him to win Desdemona, and upon learning of the marriage, Roderigo confronts Iago, whom he assumes knew of Othello's plans.
4	*'Sblood:* literally, Christ's blood; considered a severe curse word
8	*Three great ones of the city:* three important Venetian noblemen
9	*suit:* a petition; a request or plea; *lieutenant:* literally, somebody acting in place of a superior officer—in this case, a second-in-command
10	*Off-capp'd to him:* took off their hats before Othello as a gesture of respect
11	*price:* worth or value; *place:* rank or position in the hierarchy
13	*bombast circumstance:* Bombast was a substance used for stuffing quilts, thus the term means full of exaggerated details about nothing of substance.
16	*Nonsuits:* rejects the suit of; *Certes:* certainly
19	*Forsooth:* in truth; *arithmetician:* a person skilled at working with numbers; a military theorist; perhaps a "textbook" person without practical skills
21	*A fellow ... wife:* perhaps a reference to Cassio being almost married to Bianca
22	*never set a squadron:* never "set" or commanded even a small group of men in the field of battle
23	*division of a battle:* army organization
24	*spinster:* a spinner (not our current sense of the term); *unless:* except for; *bookish theoric:* theories of war learned from a book
25	*toged consuls:* wearing togas as in Roman times; a reference to the Venetian senators; *propose:* discuss or speak about
27	*had th' election:* was the person elected or chosen

Act 1, Scene 1

Venice. A street.
Enter Roderigo and Iago.

Roderigo: Tush, never tell me! I take it much unkindly
    That thou, Iago, who hast had my purse
    As if the strings were thine, shouldst know of this.
Iago: 'Sblood, but you will not hear me!
    If ever I did dream of such a matter,   5
    Abhor me.
Roderigo: Thou told'st me thou didst hold him in thy hate.
Iago: Despise me if I do not. Three great ones of the city,
    In personal suit to make me his lieutenant,
    Off-capp'd to him; and, by the faith of man,   10
    I know my price; I am worth no worse a place.
    But he, as loving his own pride and purposes,
    Evades them, with a bombast circumstance
    Horribly stuff'd with epithets of war;
    And, in conclusion,   15
    Nonsuits my mediators; for, "Certes," says he,
    "I have already chose my officer."
    And what was he?
    Forsooth, a great arithmetician,
    One Michael Cassio, a Florentine,   20
    A fellow almost damn'd in a fair wife,
    That never set a squadron in the field
    Nor the division of a battle knows
    More than a spinster; unless the bookish theoric,
    Wherein the toged consuls can propose   25
    As masterly as he. Mere prattle without practice
    Is all his soldiership. But he, sir, had th' election;
    And I, of whom his eyes had seen the proof

29	*At Rhodes, at Cyprus:* islands that the Venetians were attempting to keep within their empire
30	*be-lee'd and calm'd:* impeded in progress; nautical terms. The lee is the side where there is no wind and is thus the unfavourable side.
31	*By debitor and creditor:* a bookkeeper; *counter-caster:* a person who used counters in the process of calculating figures
32	*in good time:* as things work out, "no question"
33	*God bless the mark:* a curse expressing extreme irritation; *his Moorship:* a sarcastic reference to "his worship"; *ancient:* the lowest-ranking officer
35	*service:* serving under others, as in military service
36	*Preferment:* preferential treatment and therefore promotion; *letter:* of recommendation; *affection:* favouritism
37–38	*old gradation ... the first:* seniority. The second officer normally succeeded the first officer when he was promoted.
39	*affined:* bound or obligated to
44	*mark:* notice or observe
45	*knee-crooking knave:* a person who bows to superiors. A knave is someone who is dishonest and unprincipled and does things only for his own advancement.
48	*provender:* animal feed; *cashier'd:* dismissed from service with disgrace
49	*Whip me:* roughly means "forget that!" or "that's not for me!"
50	*trimm'd ... duty:* appearing dutiful in the way they look and behave. "Trimmed" means dressed.
52	*throwing ... service on:* making great outward shows of service toward
54	*Do themselves homage:* serve only themselves. "Homage" means respect.

59–60	*not ... seeming so:* I appear to follow him out of love and duty, though I do not.
60	*peculiar end:* the things I want to accomplish
62	*The native ... heart:* what I really intend to do
63	*In compliment extern:* in what I show outwardly
63–64	*'tis ... But:* not long after that

At Rhodes, at Cyprus, and on other grounds

Christian and heathen, must be be-lee'd and calm'd   30

By debitor and creditor; this counter-caster,

He, in good time, must his lieutenant be,

And I—God bless the mark!—his Moorship's ancient.

Roderigo: By heaven, I rather would have been his hangman.

Iago: Why, there's no remedy; 'tis the curse of service.   35

Preferment goes by letter and affection,

And not by old gradation, where each second

Stood heir to the first. Now, sir, be judge yourself,

Whether I in any just term am affined

To love the Moor.

Roderigo: I would not follow him then.   40

Iago: O, sir, content you;

I follow him to serve my turn upon him. *we don't have to follow him to be*

We cannot all be masters, nor all masters *a master*

Cannot be truly follow'd. You shall mark

Many a duteous and knee-crooking knave   45

That doting on his own obsequious bondage

Wears out his time, much like his master's ass,

For naught but provender; and when he's old, cashier'd. *as he's older he will be dismissed*

Whip me such honest knaves! Others there are

Who, trimm'd in forms and visages of duty, *they serve only* 50

Keep yet their hearts attending on themselves, *themselves*

And throwing but shows of service on their lords

Do well thrive by them, and when they have lined their coats

Do themselves homage. These fellows have some soul;

And such a one do I profess myself. For, sir,   55

It is as sure as you are Roderigo,

Were I the Moor, I would not be Iago.

In following him, I follow but myself;

Heaven is my judge, not I for love and duty,

But seeming so, for my peculiar end;   60

For when my outward action doth demonstrate

The native act and figure of my heart

In compliment extern, 'tis not long after

But I will wear my heart upon my sleeve

65	*daws:* jackdaws, a type of crow known for thievery
66	*owe:* own
67	*Carry't thus:* carry off the marriage successfully; *Call up:* wake up
68	*Make after him:* hunt down Othello
69	*Proclaim him:* identify him as a public enemy or wanted man
70–71	*though ... with flies:* Though he is now untouched, pester him with a plague of flies (biblical reference).
72	*changes:* most often printed as "chances," indicating possible things to happen
72–73	*vexation ... colour:* cause him discomfort so that his present happiness will turn unpleasant and uncomfortable
75	*like timorous accent:* literally, like the beating of loud drums to cause him dismay and discomfort
76	*by:* in the time of
80	*bags:* money-bags (so you don't get robbed)
82	*this terrible summons:* "Terrible" literally means terrifying, therefore, frightening.
85	*wherefore ... this:* "Wherefore" means why.
86	*'Zounds:* by God's wounds; a mild curse
88	*very now:* at this particular moment
89	*tupping:* mating with. A tup is a male sheep; to tup refers to the mating of a ram and ewe.
90	*snorting:* an unpleasant reference to snoring in one's sleep and therefore sounding quite undignified

For daws to peck at; I am not what I am.   65
Roderigo: What a full fortune does the thick-lips owe
  If he can carry't thus!
Iago: Call up her father,
  Rouse him. Make after him, poison his delight,
  Proclaim him in the streets. Incense her kinsmen,
  And though he in a fertile climate dwell,   70
  Plague him with flies; though that his joy be joy,
  Yet throw such changes of vexation on't
  As it may lose some colour.
Roderigo: Here is her father's house. I'll call aloud.
Iago: Do, with like timorous accent and dire yell   75
  As when, by night and negligence, the fire
  Is spied in populous cities.
Roderigo: What, ho, Brabantio! Signior Brabantio, ho!
Iago: Awake! What, ho, Brabantio! Thieves! thieves!
  Look to your house, your daughter, and your bags!   80
  Thieves! thieves!

  [*Brabantio appears above at a window.*]

Brabantio: What is the reason of this terrible summons?
  What is the matter there?
Roderigo: Signior, is all your family within?
Iago: Are your doors lock'd?
Brabantio: Why, wherefore ask you this?   85
Iago: 'Zounds, sir, you're robb'd! For shame, put on your gown!
  Your heart is burst; you have lost half your soul.
  Even now, now, very now, an old black ram
  Is tupping your white ewe. Arise, arise!
  Awake the snorting citizens with the bell,   90
  Or else the devil will make a grandsire of you.
  Arise, I say!
Brabantio: What, have you lost your wits?
Roderigo: Most reverend signior, do you know my voice?
Brabantio: Not I. What are you?
Roderigo: My name is Roderigo.
Brabantio: The worser welcome!   95

| 96 | *charged:* ordered, commanded |

99	*distempering draughts:* "Distempering" means losing the senses. The reference has to do with drinking too much alcohol, undoubtedly wine.
100	*Upon:* driven by; *bravery:* irrational anger
101	*start:* disturb or upset; *quiet:* referring to sleep
103	*place:* social position or rank

| 106 | *grange:* a country house prone to burglary because of its isolation |
| 107 | *simple:* honest, open, sincere |

110–111	*your daughter ... horse:* literally "covered" by a horse, that is, mating with a horse. "Barbary" means Moorish.
111	*nephews:* grandchildren—part of the same insult
112	*coursers:* fast horses, usually stallions; *cousins:* relatives
112–113	*gennets for germans:* small Spanish horses introduced into Spain by the Moors. "Germans" refers to close relatives.
114	*profane:* blasphemous, irreverent, or foul-mouthed
116	*making ... backs:* engaging in the sex act
118	*answer:* respond to or answer for

122	*odd-even ... night:* the time between midnight and 1:00 A.M., thus neither night nor morning. "Dull" means senseless, as in sleeping.
124	*But with ... gondolier:* then a servant giving himself for hire to anyone who wants him. Gondoliers were reputed to be agents of intrigue, so the implication is that Brabantio should be horrified that his daughter might have such an untrustworthy guard at night.
126	*your allowance:* done with your approval
127	*saucy:* impudent or insulting

I have charged thee not to haunt about my doors.
In honest plainness thou hast heard me say
My daughter is not for thee; and now, in madness,
Being full of supper and distempering draughts,
Upon malicious bravery dost thou come   100
To start my quiet.
Roderigo: Sir, sir, sir—
Brabantio: But thou must needs be sure
My spirit and my place have in them power
To make this bitter to thee.
Roderigo: Patience, good sir.
Brabantio: What tell'st thou me of robbing? This is Venice;   105
My house is not a grange.
Roderigo: Most grave Brabantio,
In simple and pure soul I come to you.
Iago: 'Zounds, sir, you are one of those that will not serve God
if the devil bid you. Because we come to do you service
and you think we are ruffians, you'll have your daughter   110
covered with a Barbary horse; you'll have your nephews
neigh to you; you'll have coursers for cousins, and gennets
for germans.
Brabantio: What profane wretch art thou?
Iago: I am one, sir, that comes to tell you your daughter and the   115
Moor are now making the beast with two backs.
Brabantio: Thou art a villain.
Iago: You are—a senator.
Brabantio: This thou shalt answer. I know thee, Roderigo.
Roderigo: Sir, I will answer anything. But I beseech you,
If't be your pleasure and most wise consent,   120
As partly I find it is, that your fair daughter,
At this odd-even and dull watch o' the night,
Transported, with no worse nor better guard
But with a knave of common hire, a gondolier,
To the gross clasps of a lascivious Moor—   125
If this be known to you, and your allowance,
We then have done you bold and saucy wrongs;
But if you know not this, my manners tell me

He's implying that
his daughter has such an escort
should be disgusted.

15

130	*from ... civility:* contrary to what is fitting or proper
133	*gross revolt:* an indecent or unthinkable rebellion
134	*wit:* intelligence

135–136	*In ... everywhere:* to an inconstant or unreliable stranger who wanders aimlessly, with no fixed address
136	*Straight ... yourself:* figure out what is really going on

139	*Strike ... tinder:* light the inflammable material. Tinder is the material used to spark a fire when flint is struck on steel.
140	*taper:* candle, or, more likely, a torch
141	*accident:* something unexpected; here, Desdemona's unexpected and sudden marriage

144–146	*It seems ... Against the Moor:* It is not fitting for a person in my position to be discovered undermining him or turning him in. *state:* the duke
147	*gall:* annoy or bother; *check:* rebuke, protest, or censure
148	*cast:* dismiss
148–149	*embark'd ... reason:* suddenly and urgently involved in
150	*stand in act:* about to happen or are in progress; *for their souls:* even if they paid with their souls
151	*of his fathom:* with his ability or capacity as a military leader; literally, a measure of depth
154	*life:* livelihood
155	*flag:* a sign of welcome
156	*That:* meaning "so that"
157	*Sagittary:* probably the name of an inn or tavern displaying the sign of the centaur archer, as in Sagittarius (ninth sign of the zodiac); *search:* search party; Stage Direction: *nightgown*—likely a dressing-gown or robe
160	*what's ... time:* what remains of my now worthless and miserable life

We have your wrong rebuke. Do not believe
That, from the sense of all civility,   130
I thus would play and trifle with your reverence.
Your daughter, if you have not given her leave,
I say again, hath made a gross revolt,
Tying her duty, beauty, wit, and fortunes
In an extravagant and wheeling stranger   135
Of here and everywhere. Straight satisfy yourself.
If she be in her chamber, or your house,
Let loose on me the justice of the state
For thus deluding you.
Brabantio: Strike on the tinder, ho!
Give me a taper! Call up all my people!   140
This accident is not unlike my dream.
Belief of it oppresses me already.
Light, I say! light!   [*Exit above.*]
Iago: Farewell, for I must leave you.
It seems not meet, nor wholesome to my place,
To be produced—as, if I stay, I shall—   145
Against the Moor. For I do know the state,
However this may gall him with some check,
Cannot with safety cast him; for he's embark'd
With such loud reason to the Cyprus wars,
Which even now stand in act, that for their souls   150
Another of his fathom they have none
To lead their business; in which regard,
Though I do hate him as I do hell pains,
Yet, for necessity of present life,
I must show out a flag and sign of love,   155
Which is indeed but sign. That you shall surely find him,
Lead to the Sagittary the raised search;
And there will I be with him. So farewell.   [*Exit.*]
[*Enter below Brabantio, in his nightgown, and Servants*
     with torches.]
Brabantio: It is too true an evil. Gone she is;
And what's to come of my despised time   160
Is naught but bitterness. Now, Roderigo,

165	*Past thought:* beyond understanding; *moe:* more
166	*Raise:* wake up

168	*treason of the blood:* treachery or deceit of one's own child; also, literally, the uncontrolled riot of the passions which, when in check, govern the rational behaviour of a person
169	*from hence:* from this time forward
170–172	*Is there not ... May be abused:* Aren't there magic spells that cause a young girl to go astray? *property:* nature or character; *abused:* tricked or deceived; possibly, violated

177	*discover:* find

180	*I ... most:* Based on my status, I can get assistance from just about anybody.
181	*special officers of night:* the guardians of the city at night; special night-police
182	*deserve:* reward

Where didst thou see her? O unhappy girl!
With the Moor, say'st thou?—Who would be a father?—
How didst thou know 'twas she? O, she deceives me
Past thought! What said she to you? Get moe tapers!   165
Raise all my kindred! Are they married, think you?
Roderigo: Truly I think they are.
Brabantio: O heaven! How got she out? O treason of the blood!
Fathers, from hence trust not your daughters' minds
By what you see them act. Is there not charms   170
By which the property of youth and maidhood
May be abused? Have you not read, Roderigo,
Of some such thing?
Roderigo: Yes, sir, I have indeed.
Brabantio: Call up my brother. O, would you had had her!
Some one way, some another. Do you know   175
Where we may apprehend her and the Moor?
Roderigo: I think I can discover him, if you please
To get good guard and go along with me.
Brabantio: Pray you lead on. At every house I'll call;
I may command at most. Get weapons, ho!   180
And raise some special officers of night.
On, good Roderigo; I'll deserve your pains.   [*Exeunt.*]

Act 1, Scene 1: Activities

1. The play begins with an argument. With your group, suggest what such a beginning might imply for the rest of the play. What are the people involved arguing about? In your group, discuss how you might respond to these people. What do you think about petty arguments?

2. Thwarted ambition seems to be one source of Iago's discontent. In your group, discuss what it is that Iago actually wants, and determine why he is so angry. In your journal, write an account of an ambition that you had that wasn't fulfilled. How did you react? What was the outcome? What advice might you offer to others about the perils of being consumed by ambition?

3. We know nothing at all about Roderigo in concrete terms. Write a character sketch of this man as a film director might view him. Describe him in a way that would help the actor you have hired to play this part.

4. What are your views on elopement? Why do people choose to elope? What seem to be Desdemona's reasons for doing so? Discuss with your group what her own Venetian society and an Elizabethan audience might think of such an act. Are modern views on this topic different? What evidence can you give to support your opinion?

5. There is little evidence to suggest what the setting for this scene might look like. With a partner or with your group, create what you think would be an effective opening set for the play. You can sketch your ideas or describe them orally. Why is a striking opening set important to a play?

6. Iago seems to be vehemently angry. The source of his anger isn't fully apparent, but it may have to do with his rejection by Othello in favour of Cassio. Write a short soliloquy in which Iago reveals how he feels and what he is thinking about.

7. First impressions are often lasting ones. What are your impressions of Brabantio? Draw a picture or cartoon to

illustrate how you imagine him. Do you think he is a likeable character, or not? What sort of relationship do you suppose he had with his daughter?

8. There is talk of "charms" and sorcery concerning Othello's "conquest" of Desdemona. Do you think such things are possible? Think of a movie or soap opera where such things appeared to happen. How can one person be "charmed" by another? On what grounds does Brabantio make such accusations? Do you believe him? Why does he say such things?

9. We have yet to meet Desdemona. What are your impressions of her, given what you know about her so far? How valid do you think one person's opinion about the character of another is? Keep an account of Desdemona's actions as the play progresses so that you can make your own assessment of her at the end. Are people ever really what they appear to be? Write a journal entry expressing your views on the subject.

For the next scene ...

When you encounter people who do not agree with your point of view about a particular issue, what do you do? Ignore them? Try to convince them that you are right? Feel somehow insignificant? Get angry? Do nothing?

Act 1, Scene 2

In this scene ...

Iago tells Othello what Roderigo has done and warns him of Brabantio's resulting rage. Othello, however, feels certain that his loyalty and service to Venice, combined with his genuine love for Desdemona, will prove stronger than Brabantio's outraged accusations. A group of the Duke's officers enters, along with Othello's new lieutenant, Cassio. Cassio tells Othello that the Duke urgently requires his presence. News has arrived that the Turks (enemies of Venice) are about to attack the island of Cyprus, a Venetian colony. On their way, the group meets Brabantio and his search party who have come to arrest Othello. Brabantio accuses Othello of using magic and other illegal means to win over his daughter, and he demands justice. Othello manages to avoid a street fight and to convince Brabantio to go with him and to state his case against him before the Duke and his council. They all move on to present themselves in the Duke's council chamber.

2	*stuff o' the conscience:* a matter of conscience
3	*contrived:* deliberate; *iniquity:* wickedness
5	*yerk'd:* stabbed; *him:* Iago is speaking of Roderigo and pretending to relate what he has done and said against Othello.
6	*prated:* spoke insolently
7	*scurvy:* uncomplimentary, insulting
10	*I did ... him:* I had difficulty keeping my hands off him.
11	*fast:* firmly, securely
12	*the magnifico:* the title given to a wealthy Venetian nobleman of the highest rank, in this case Brabantio
13–14	*And hath in his effect ... the Duke's:* is potentially twice as powerful as the Duke; that is, Brabantio can be as effective as the Duke
15	*grievance:* oppression
16	*might ... on:* power to enforce it fully
17	*cable:* rope; that is, scope or range
18	*signiory:* the rulers of Venice
19	*out-tongue:* override; *'Tis ... know:* It is as yet unknown.
21	*promulgate:* proclaim; *fetch ... being:* am descended
22	*siege:* rank; *demerits:* merits or worthiness
23–24	*May ... reach'd:* My worthy acts give me a status equal to that of Desdemona's family.
25	*But that:* except for the fact that
26	*unhoused:* literally "homeless"; unconfined

Scene 2

Another street.

Enter Othello, Iago, and
Attendants with torches.

Iago: Though in the trade of war I have slain men,
   Yet do I hold it very stuff o' the conscience
   To do no contrived murder. I lack iniquity
   Sometimes to do me service. Nine or ten times
   I had thought to have yerk'd him here under the ribs.   5
Othello: 'Tis better as it is.
Iago: Nay, but he prated,
   And spoke such scurvy and provoking terms
   Against your honour
   That with the little godliness I have
   I did full hard forbear him. But I pray you, sir,   10
   Are you fast married? Be assured of this,
   That the magnifico is much beloved,
   And hath in his effect a voice potential
   As double as the Duke's. He will divorce you,
   Or put upon you what restraint and grievance   15
   The law, with all his might to enforce it on,
   Will give him cable.
Othello: Let him do his spite.
   My services which I have done the signiory
   Shall out-tongue his complaints. 'Tis yet to know—
   Which, when I know that boasting is an honour,   20
   I shall promulgate—I fetch my life and being
   From men of royal siege; and my demerits
   May speak unbonneted to as proud a fortune
   As this that I have reach'd. For know, Iago,
   But that I love the gentle Desdemona,   25
   I would not my unhoused free condition

27	*circumscription and confine:* restraint and confinement
28	*sea's worth:* all the treasures the sea contains
29	*raised:* stirred to action, aroused
31	*parts:* abilities; *perfect soul:* stainless character
33	*Janus:* the two-headed, two-faced Roman God
37	*haste-post-haste:* immediate
38	*on the instant:* right away
40	*heat:* urgency; *galleys:* sailing ships
41	*sequent:* successive
43	*consuls:* senators
44	*hotly:* urgently
46	*several:* separate
49	*what makes he:* what is he doing
50	*boarded:* went aboard; *carack:* treasure ship. Note the sexual innuendo.
51	*prize:* plunder or prize; *made:* rich
53	*Marry:* by the Virgin Mary

Put into circumscription and confine
For the sea's worth. But look, what lights come yond?

[*Enter Cassio and certain Officers with torches.*]

Iago: Those are the raised father and his friends;
  You were best go in.
Othello: Not I; I must be found.   30
  My parts, my title, and my perfect soul
  Shall manifest me rightly. Is it they?
Iago: By Janus, I think no.
Othello: The servants of the Duke, and my lieutenant.
  The goodness of the night upon you, friends!   35
  What is the news?
Cassio: The Duke does greet you, general;
  And he requires your haste-post-haste appearance
  Even on the instant.
Othello: What's the matter, think you?
Cassio: Something from Cyprus, as I may divine.
  It is a business of some heat. The galleys   40
  Have sent a dozen sequent messengers
  This very night at one another's heels,
  And many of the consuls, raised and met,
  Are at the Duke's already. You have been hotly call'd for;
  When, being not at your lodging to be found,   45
  The Senate hath sent about three several quests
  To search you out.
Othello: 'Tis well I am found by you.
  I will but spend a word here in the house,
  And go with you.   [*Exit.*]
Cassio: Ancient, what makes he here?
Iago: Faith, he to-night hath boarded a land carack.   50
  If it prove lawful prize, he's made for ever.
Cassio: I do not understand.
Iago: He's married.
Cassio: To who?

  [*Re-enter Othello.*]

Iago: Marry, to—Come captain, will you go?

53	*Have with you:* I shall go with you.
55	*advised:* cautious
56	*to:* with; *stand:* stop
58	*I am for you:* a challenge to fight
59	*Keep up:* put away, sheathe; *bright:* unused
63	*enchanted:* bewitched or charmed
64	*I'll … sense:* base my argument on all ordinary understanding of nature, that is, evidence clear to the senses
66	*tender:* young
67	*opposite:* opposed
68	*curled:* Elizabethan men of fashion often wore "a curled bush of frizzled hair."
69	*a general mock:* public scorn, derision, or shame
70	*guardage:* guardianship
71	*such a thing … to delight:* You are someone who would cause a maiden fear rather than delight.
72	*Judge me the world:* Let the world judge me. *gross in sense:* obvious or self-evident
73	*practised on her:* used trickery
75	*motion:* emotion; *disputed on:* argued in the courts
77	*attach:* arrest
79	*arts … warrant:* forbidden and illegal acts, practising magic
80	*Lay hold:* stop or restrain
82	*you of my inclining:* my followers
84	*Where will you that I go:* Where do you want me to go?

Othello: Have with you.

Cassio: Here comes another troop to seek for you.

   [*Enter Brabantio, Roderigo, and Officers with torches and weapons.*]

Iago: It is Brabantio. General, be advised.   55
   He comes to bad intent.

Othello: Holla! stand there!

Roderigo: Signior, it is the Moor.

Brabantio: Down with him, thief!
                       [*They draw on both sides.*]

Iago: You, Roderigo! Come, sir, I am for you.

Othello: Keep up your bright swords, for the dew will rust them.
   Good signior, you shall more command with years   60
   Than with your weapons.

Brabantio: O thou foul thief, where hast thou stow'd my daughter?
   Damn'd as thou art, thou hast enchanted her!
   For I'll refer me to all things of sense,
   If she in chains of magic were not bound,   65
   Whether a maid so tender, fair, and happy,
   So opposite to marriage that she shunn'd
   The wealthy curled darlings of our nation,
   Would ever have, to incur a general mock,
   Run from her guardage to the sooty bosom   70
   Of such a thing as thou, to fear, not to delight.
   Judge me the world if 'tis not gross in sense
   That thou hast practised on her with foul charms,
   Abused her delicate youth with drugs or minerals
   That weaken motion. I'll have't disputed on;   75
   'Tis probable, and palpable to thinking.
   I therefore apprehend and do attach thee
   For an abuser of the world, a practiser
   Of arts inhibited and out of warrant.
   Lay hold upon him. If he do resist,   80
   Subdue him at his peril.

Othello: Hold your hands,
   Both you of my inclining and the rest.
   Were it my cue to fight, I should have known it
   Without a prompter. Where will you that I go

85–87   *till ... answer:* until the law court holds its next session, perhaps one specially arranged

90   *present:* immediate

95   *idle:* trivial

98   *may ... free:* are freely permitted
99   *pagans:* a term of contempt

To answer this your charge?
Brabantio: To prison, till fit time   85
   Of law and course of direct session
   Call thee to answer.
Othello: *What if I do obey?*
   How may the Duke be therewith satisfied,
   Whose messengers are here about my side
   Upon some present business of the state   90
   To bring me to him?
Officer: 'Tis true, most worthy signior.
   The Duke's in council, and your noble self
   I am sure is sent for.
Brabantio: How! The Duke in council!
   In this time of the night! Bring him away.
   Mine's not an idle cause. The Duke himself,   95
   Or any of my brothers of the state,
   Cannot but feel this wrong as 'twere their own;
   For if such actions may have passage free,
   Bond-slaves and pagans shall our statesmen be.   [*Exeunt.*]

Act 1, Scene 2: Activities

1. As this scene opens, certain events have apparently occurred since the previous scene. Discuss with your group what has probably transpired. You might consider

   - the motivation for Iago's opening speech—what might have happened to make him say such things?
   - Iago's protestations that his conscience won't allow him to do "contrived murder"
   - Brabantio's crazed accusations against Othello in Scene 1
   - Iago's declarations of loyalty to Othello (a man he says he hates) in this scene
   - Othello's responses to Iago's apparent anger and concern for Othello's safety
   - Othello's replies to Iago and what you consider to be his rationale for making such statements

2. Recreate the scene in the Sagittary Inn where Othello and Desdemona are found by Brabantio's search party. Why would a military man of considerable stature choose to celebrate his marriage in a pub? What do you envision the pub scene to be like? You could stage your version for the class.

3. Othello is a career soldier, unaccustomed to peacetime society, and he counts his worth by his loyalty to the state. When he is summoned by the Duke and then confronted by Brabantio and Roderigo, he seems puzzled by the charge against him. As a Venetian newspaper reporter, write your account of what happened on the street that night. As a reporter, you are aware of possible difficulties with the Turkish, who have designs on Venetian-held Cyprus. Decide whether your account should emphasize this or the confrontation between Brabantio and Othello.

   Remember to capture your reader's interest with a headline and an intriguing first paragraph. You might want to look at several newspaper articles to make sure your format is effective.

4. How do you account for Brabantio's outrage? Given the social context, how would you react as a father? If you could speak to

32

him, what advice would you offer? If he listened to you at all, do you think your advice would have any effect on him? Why or why not? Use this incident as a subject for a speech to a group of concerned parents who feel that their children have disobeyed them. Remember, a clear theme is very important. Before you write the speech, think about the reaction you wish to elicit from the audience. You could present your final version to the class for their reaction.

5. This may be a tricky scene to stage. Scene 1 tells us that Othello and Desdemona are at the Sagittary Inn, yet Scene 2 opens on a street. In your opinion, where do the confrontations actually take place? Create the stage directions you would use for filming Scene 2. Discuss your directions with other groups or with the class. Decide how important staging is to the success of a scene.

6. Why do you think Othello was not introduced in the first scene, even though the play bears his name? How important do you think his reputation as a great soldier is to his overall social standing? Since this is your first encounter with Othello, what are your impressions of him? Keep an ongoing record of your impressions to see if Othello changes as the play progresses.

7. Create a soliloquy for Iago that might end this scene. Remember that a soliloquy is a speech delivered by one person to himself revealing his innermost thoughts about a subject or events. What subjects do you think Iago would include in his speech, based on what we already know about him? You may wish to discuss this with your group before you begin writing.

For the next scene ...

When is the first time you realized that people are not always what they appear to be? How did this realization change your attitude about people and the way you deal with them?

Act 1, Scene 3

In this scene ...

At the council meeting, the Duke and senators discuss the tactics of the Turkish fleet and decide that the fleet's final destination is most likely Cyprus. When Brabantio and Othello arrive, the Duke addresses Othello about the crisis while Brabantio immediately focuses on his personal grudge against Othello, accusing him again of using "charms" and magic in his conquest of Desdemona. The Duke demands proof of the charges, and Othello suggests that Desdemona be summoned to tell her side of the story. Before she arrives, Othello describes his relationship with and courtship of her. When she enters, she tells her father and the assembled group that her marriage was entirely based on her love for Othello. The Duke believes her and vindicates Othello. Brabantio has no choice but to give up his quest for justice, and he bitterly withdraws. The council then proceeds with the pressing matter of the imminent attack on Cyprus, and Othello is placed in charge of this emergency military operation. Desdemona is placed in the trust of Iago and his wife, Emilia, who are to follow Othello to Cyprus. Roderigo, now alone with Iago, threatens suicide at his loss of Desdemona, but Iago talks him out of it, admonishing him to "be a man." Iago then convinces Roderigo that the situation between Othello and Desdemona may well change over time, and that Roderigo should sell all his property in order to raise more money to follow them to Cyprus in pursuit of her affections. Iago now plans to involve Cassio in his scheme by hinting to Othello that the handsome lieutenant is too friendly with Desdemona. If this plan succeeds, Iago will be able to get revenge on Othello and at the same time discredit Cassio, obtaining his position as lieutenant.

1–2   *There is no ... credit:* There is no consistency in these
        reports that gives them credibility.

5   *jump ... account:* do not agree on the precise number
6   *aim:* guess or estimate

8   *and bearing up to:* approaching

10–12   *I do ... sense:* The numbers disagree in the reports, but I
        am certain that the main body of information (that the
        Turkish fleet is sailing) is frighteningly true.

14   *preparation:* the fleet of warships

17   *How ... change:* What do you think about this change?
18   *By no assay of reason:* by any reasonable test
19   *in false gaze:* looking the wrong way

Scene 3

A council-chamber.
The Duke and Senators sitting at
a table; Officers attending.

Duke: There is no composition in these news
   That gives them credit.
First Senator: Indeed they are disproportion'd.
   My letters say a hundred and seven galleys.
Duke: And mine a hundred and forty.
Second Senator: And mine, two hundred.
   But though they jump not on a just account—   5
   As in these cases, where the aim reports,
   'Tis oft with difference—yet do they all confirm
   A Turkish fleet, and bearing up to Cyprus.
Duke: Nay, it is possible enough to judgement.
   I do not so secure me in the error   10
   But the main article I do approve
   In fearful sense.
Sailor: [*Within.*]   What, ho! what, ho! what, ho!
Officer: A messenger from the galleys.

   [*Enter Sailor.*]

Duke: Now, what's the business?
Sailor: The Turkish preparation makes for Rhodes.
   So was I bid report here to the state   15
   By Signior Angelo.
Duke: How say you by this change?
First Senator: This cannot be
   By no assay of reason. 'Tis a pageant
   To keep us in false gaze. When we consider
   The importancy of Cyprus to the Turk,   20
   And let ourselves again but understand
   That as it more concerns the Turk than Rhodes,

23	*with ... it:* more easily capture it (Cyprus); *question:* contest
24	*brace:* state of defence. A brace was armour to protect the arm.
26	*dress'd in:* equipped with
28	*latest:* to the last
30	*wake and wage:* arouse and risk
33	*Ottomites:* Turks; *reverend and gracious:* addressed to the Duke
35	*injointed:* joined; *an after:* following, second
37–38	*re-stem ... course:* retrace their route; *with frank appearance:* openly
40	*servitor:* servant
41	*With ... thus:* with all due respect advises you
44	*Marcus Luccicos ... town:* Isn't Marcus in town?
46	*post, post-haste:* as quickly as possible; *dispatch:* with speed
48	*straight:* immediately
48–49	*employ you ... Ottoman:* It was the policy of the Venetian state to employ strangers, and even Moors, in their wars. Putting such people in command of armies ensured that Venetians would not be put at risk and that no Venetian general or captain would decide to use his army to overthrow the state, as Caesar had.
53	*place:* official position; *aught:* anything
55	*particular:* personal
56	*floodgate:* torrential

So may he with more facile question bear it,
For that it stands not in such warlike brace,
But altogether lacks the abilities   25
That Rhodes is dress'd in—if we make thought of this,
We must not think the Turk is so unskilful
To leave that latest which concerns him first,
Neglecting an attempt of ease and gain
To wake and wage a danger profitless.   30
Duke: Nay, in all confidence he's not for Rhodes.
Officer: Here is more news.

   [*Enter a Messenger.*]

Messenger: The Ottomites, reverend and gracious,
   Steering with due course toward the isle of Rhodes,
   Have there injointed them with an after fleet.   35
First Senator: Ay, so I thought. How many, as you guess?
Messenger: Of thirty sail; and now they do re-stem
   Their backward course, bearing with frank appearance
   Their purposes toward Cyprus. Signior Montano,
   Your trusty and most valiant servitor,   40
   With his free duty recommends you thus,
   And prays you to believe him.
Duke: 'Tis certain then for Cyprus.
   Marcus Luccicos, is not he in town?
First Senator: He's now in Florence.   45
Duke: Write from us to him; post, post-haste dispatch.
First Senator: Here comes Brabantio and the valiant Moor.

   [*Enter Brabantio, Othello, Cassio, Iago, Roderigo, and Officers.*]

Duke: Valiant Othello, we must straight employ you
   Against the general enemy Ottoman.
   [*To Brabantio.*] I did not see you. Welcome, gentle signior.   50
   We lack'd your counsel and your help to-night.
Brabantio: So did I yours. Good your grace, pardon me.
   Neither my place, nor aught I heard of business,
   Hath raised me from my bed; nor doth the general care
   Take hold on me; for my particular grief   55
   Is of so floodgate and o'erbearing nature

57	*engluts:* engulfs, swallows
61	*mountebanks:* imposters, quacks, frauds
62–64	*For nature ... not:* Nature could not make such a gross error without (sans) the use of witchcraft because it is not feeble-minded nor incapacitated in any way.
66	*beguiled ... herself:* cheated your daughter of herself; that is, caused her to behave as she normally wouldn't
67	*the bloody book of law:* Under Venetian law, to give love potions was highly criminal and warranted the death penalty.
68–69	*You ... sense:* You shall judge and impose sentence in terms of your own interpretation (sense) of the law.
69	*proper:* own
70	*Stood ... action:* were the person charged
74	*in your own part:* on your own behalf
75	*but:* except
77	*approved good:* proved by experience to be good
80	*The very ... offending:* the most obvious of my offences; *front:* forehead
81	*Rude:* unpolished, blunt
83	*pith:* marrow, hence strength
84	*some ... wasted:* nine months ago, From when he was seven until very recently (nine months ago) he has been a soldier.
85	*dearest:* most significant or worthy; *tented field:* the battle-field filled with army tents

That it engluts and swallows other sorrows,
  And it is still itself.
Duke: Why, what's the matter?
Brabantio: My daughter! O, my daughter!
All: Dead?
Brabantio: Ay, to me.
  She is abused, stol'n from me, and corrupted   60
  By spells and medicines bought of mountebanks;
  For nature so preposterously to err,
  Being not deficient, blind, or lame of sense,
  Sans witchcraft could not.
Duke: Whoe'er he be that in this foul proceeding   65
  Hath thus beguiled your daughter of herself
  And you of her, the bloody book of law
  You shall yourself read in the bitter letter
  After your own sense; yea, though our proper son
  Stood in your action.
Brabantio: Humbly I thank your grace.   70
  Here is the man, this Moor, whom now, it seems,
  Your special mandate for the state affairs
  Hath hither brought.
All: We are very sorry for't.
Duke [*To Othello.*] What, in your own part, can you say to this?
Brabantio: Nothing, but this is so.   75
Othello: Most potent, grave, and reverend signiors,
  My very noble, and approved good masters,
  That I have ta'en away this old man's daughter,
  It is most true; true I have married her.
  The very head and front of my offending   80
  Hath this extent, no more. Rude am I in my speech,
  And little blest with the soft phrase of peace;
  For since these arms of mine had seven years' pith
  Till now some nine moons wasted, they have used
  Their dearest action in the tented field;   85
  And little of this great world can I speak
  More than pertains to feats of broil and battle;
  And therefore little shall I grace my cause

90　　　　*round unvarnish'd tale:* plain or blunt, unembellished account

93　　　　*withal:* with

95–96　　*her motion ... herself:* She was so modest that her emotions made her blush at just about anything.

97　　　　*credit:* reputation

101　　　*must be driven:* must be pressured
102　　　*practices ... hell:* clever hellish plots

104　　　*mixtures:* of drugs; *blood:* passions
105　　　*dram ... effect:* a dose of liquid charmed by incantations for this purpose

107　　　*Without ... test:* without more complete and comprehensive, clear evidence; *overt:* open

108　　　*thin habits:* sketchy evidence. The reference is to light clothing of little substance; "habits" refers to apparel.

109　　　*modern seeming:* commonplace or ordinary appearance; *prefer:* produce or bring forward (as in accusation); that is, the evidence is merely circumstantial

111　　　*forced courses:* unnaturally forced, perhaps planned methods

113　　　*it:* Desdemona's love; *question:* talk
114　　　*affordeth:* might allow

116　　　*before:* in front of

In speaking for myself. Yet, by your gracious patience,
I will a round unvarnish'd tale deliver   90
Of my whole course of love—what drugs, what charms,
What conjuration, and what mighty magic—
For such proceeding am I charged withal—
I won his daughter.
Brabantio: A maiden never bold;
Of spirit so still and quiet that her motion   95
Blush'd at herself; and she—in spite of nature,
Of years, of country, credit, everything—
To fall in love with what she fear'd to look on!
It is a judgement maimed and most imperfect
That will confess perfection so could err   100
Against all rules of nature, and must be driven
To find out practices of cunning hell
Why this should be. I therefore vouch again
That with some mixtures powerful o'er the blood,
Or with some dram, conjured to this effect,   105
He wrought upon her.
Duke: To vouch this is no proof,
Without more certain and more overt test
Than these thin habits and poor likelihoods
Of modern seeming do prefer against him.
First Senator: But, Othello, speak.   110
Did you by indirect and forced courses
Subdue and poison this young maid's affections?
Or came it by request, and such fair question
As soul to soul affordeth?
Othello: I do beseech you,
Send for the lady to the Sagittary   115
And let her speak of me before her father.
If you do find me foul in her report,
The trust, the office, I do hold of you
Not only take away, but let your sentence
Even fall upon my life.
Duke: Fetch Desdemona hither.   120
Othello: Ancient, conduct them; you best know the place.
                              [*Exeunt Iago and Attendants.*]

123   *vices of my blood:* sins against my soul

124   *justly:* precisely

129   *Still:* frequently, often

131   *pass'd:* experienced, endured

134   *chances:* occurrences or events

135   *moving accidents:* memorable horrendous events

136   *imminent deadly breach:* a break in the fortifications that could have been fatal for all

138   *redemption:* being held for ransom, buying back

139   *portance:* conduct

140   *antres:* caverns or caves; *idle:* barren or empty

142   *hint:* opportunity; *process:* story or tale

144   *Anthropophagi:* cannibals. The word was used in Sir Walter Raleigh's account of his Guiana trip in 1595, a story the Elizabethans loved. While Sir Walter seems to have coined the term, it is mentioned in the tales of other adventurers.

151   *pliant:* convenient

153   *dilate:* recount in detail or expand

154   *by parcels:* by portions or individual pieces

155   *intentively:* with complete attention

156   *beguile her of:* draw from her

And till she come, as truly as to heaven
I do confess the vices of my blood,
So justly to your grave ears I'll present
How I did thrive in this fair lady's love,   125
And she in mine.
Duke: Say it, Othello.
Othello: Her father loved me, oft invited me,
Still question'd me the story of my life
From year to year, the battles, sieges, fortunes   130
That I have pass'd.
I ran it through, even from my boyish days
To the very moment that he bade me tell it.
Wherein I spake of most disastrous chances,
Of moving accidents by flood and field,   135
Of hairbreadth scapes i' the imminent deadly breach,
Of being taken by the insolent foe
And sold to slavery, of my redemption thence
And portance in my travel's history;
Wherein of antres vast and deserts idle,   140
Rough quarries, rocks, and hills whose heads touch heaven,
It was my hint to speak—such was the process;
And of the Cannibals that each other eat,
The Anthropophagi, and men whose heads
Do grow beneath their shoulders. This to hear   145
Would Desdemona seriously incline;
But still the house-affairs would draw her thence;
Which ever as she could with haste dispatch,
She'ld come again, and with a greedy ear
Devour up my discourse. Which I observing,   150
Took once a pliant hour, and found good means
To draw from her a prayer of earnest heart
That I would all my pilgrimage dilate,
Whereof by parcels she had something heard,
But not intentively. I did consent,   155
And often did beguile her of her tears
When I did speak of some distressful stroke

159   *sighs:* possibly "kisses"
160   *passing strange:* slang for "most strange or odd"

163   *her:* for her

170   *witness:* confirm, or give testimony or evidence

173   *Take ... best:* make the best of this confused affair

177   *Destruction ... head:* Literally, let destruction fall on my head.

182   *bound:* obliged to; *education:* the way I was brought up
183   *learn:* teach
184   *the lord of duty:* the person to whom I owe loyalty and
        obedience

188   *challenge:* claim

189   *I have done:* I am finished

That my youth suffer'd. My story being done,
She gave me for my pains a world of sighs.
She swore, in faith, 'twas strange, 'twas passing strange;   160
'Twas pitiful, 'twas wondrous pitiful.
She wish'd she had not heard it; yet she wish'd,
That heaven had made her such a man. She thank'd me,
And bade me, if I had a friend that loved her,
I should but teach him how to tell my story,   165
And that would woo her. Upon this hint I spake.
She loved me for the dangers I had pass'd,
And I loved her that she did pity them.
This only is the witchcraft I have used.
Here comes the lady. Let her witness it.   170

[*Enter Desdemona, Iago, and Attendants.*]

Duke: I think this tale would win my daughter too.
  Good Brabantio,
  Take up this mangled matter at the best.
  Men do their broken weapons rather use
  Than their bare hands.
Brabantio: I pray you hear her speak.   175
  If she confess that she was half the wooer,
  Destruction on my head if my bad blame
  Light on the man! Come hither, gentle mistress.
  Do you perceive in all this noble company
  Where most you owe obedience?
Desdemona: My noble father,   180
  I do perceive here a divided duty.
  To you I am bound for life and education;
  My life and education both do learn me
  How to respect you: you are the lord of duty;
  I am hitherto your daughter. But here's my husband,   185
  And so much duty as my mother show'd
  To you, preferring you before her father,
  So much I challenge that I may profess
  Due to the Moor my lord.
Brabantio: God be with you! I have done.
  Please it your grace, on to the state-affairs.   190

191	*get:* produce a child through procreation
197	*For ... tyranny:* Your escape (elopement) would teach me to be cruel by imposing restrictions on them.
198	*clogs:* weights to impede movement, used on horses and captives
199	*lay a sentence:* declare a general truth, a rule of conduct
200	*grise:* stage
202–203	*When ... depended:* Our fears are ended when what we are afraid of happens; what is beyond help is beyond our ability to change.
204	*mischief:* bad luck
205	*next:* the nearest; the most likely
207	*Patience ... makes:* Patience makes a joke of the harm fortune has done. *her:* fortune's
209	*spends a bootless grief:* wastes his time grieving his losses; *bootless:* profitless, useless
212–215	*He bears ... borrow:* Brabantio is making a sarcastic comparison between two possible responses to bad fortune.
216	*gall:* sour taste
219	*pierced:* possibly lanced in the medical sense, thus "treated," or Brabantio claims that his heart cannot be any more "pierced" by the useless advice the Duke suggests to him. Either reading makes sense.
222	*fortitude:* strength or defences
223	*substitute:* an appointed second-in-command
224	*allowed sufficiency:* understood and acknowledged efficiency
224–225	*yet ... you:* Yet public opinion, which governs our actions, regards you as a safer choice.
226	*slubber:* soil or stain
227–228	*stubborn and boisterous:* rough and violent

I had rather to adopt a child than get it.
Come hither, Moor.
I here do give thee that with all my heart
Which, but thou hast already, with all my heart
I would keep from thee. For your sake, jewel,   195
I am glad at soul I have no other child;
For thy escape would teach me tyranny,
To hang clogs on them. I have done, my lord.
Duke: Let me speak like yourself and lay a sentence
    Which, as a grise or step, may help these lovers   200
    Into your favour.
    When remedies are past, the griefs are ended
    By seeing the worst, which late on hopes depended.
    To mourn a mischief that is past and gone
    Is the next way to draw new mischief on.   205
    What cannot be preserved when fortune takes,
    Patience her injury a mockery makes.
    The robb'd that smiles steals something from the thief;
    He robs himself that spends a bootless grief.
Brabantio: So let the Turk of Cyprus us beguile;   210
    We lost it not so long as we can smile.
    He bears the sentence well that nothing bears
    But the free comfort which from thence he hears;
    But he bears both the sentence and the sorrow
    That, to pay grief, must of poor patience borrow.   215
    These sentences, to sugar, or to gall,
    Being strong on both sides, are equivocal.
    But words are words. I never yet did hear
    That the bruised heart was pierced through the ear.
    I humbly beseech you, proceed to the affairs of state.   220
Duke: The Turk with a most mighty preparation makes
    for Cyprus. Othello, the fortitude of the place is best
    known to you; and though we have there a substitute
    of most allowed sufficiency, yet opinion, a sovereign
    mistress of effects, throws a more safer voice on you.   225
    You must therefore be content to slubber the gloss
    of your new fortunes with this more stubborn and

229–231 *custom ... down:* I am so used to the hard beds of war that they seem soft and comfortable to me. *thrice-driven bed of down:* an exceptionally soft bed because the feathers have been air blown three times so that only the smallest and softest remain

231 *agnize:* know within myself

232–233 *alacrity ... hardness:* readiness to undergo hardship

235 *state:* position of power

236 *fit disposition:* proper or suitable arrangements

237 *Due ... exhibition:* treatment befitting her position, including residence and finances

238 *besort:* appropriate company

239 *levels ... breeding:* is suitable to her position

244 *To ... ear:* listen with understanding to my proposed plan

245–246 *And ... simpleness:* Allow me the honour of your voice to compensate for my lack of expertise as a speaker.

247 *What would you:* What would you like?

249 *My ... fortunes:* the violence and storm of fortunes that I have braved or encountered in marrying Othello

250–251 *My heart's ... lord:* My heart has become a soldier, like my husband; that is, I too would go to the wars like a soldier.

256 *moth:* an insignificant creature

258 *heavy:* tiresome or boring

260 *voices:* approval

boisterous expedition.

Othello: The tyrant custom, most grave senators,
    Hath made the flinty and steel couch of war   230
    My thrice-driven bed of down. I do agnize
    A natural and prompt alacrity
    I find in hardness; and do undertake
    These present wars against the Ottomites.
    Most humbly, therefore, bending to your state,   235
    I crave fit disposition for my wife,
    Due reference of place, and exhibition,
    With such accommodation and besort
    As levels with her breeding.

Duke: If you please,
    Be't at her father's.

Brabantio: I'll not have it so.   240

Othello: Nor I.

Desdemona: Nor I. I would not there reside,
    To put my father in impatient thoughts
    By being in his eye. Most gracious Duke,
    To my unfolding lend your prosperous ear,
    And let me find a charter in your voice,   245
    To assist my simpleness.

Duke: What would you, Desdemona?

Desdemona: That I did love the Moor to live with him,
    My downright violence and storm of fortunes
    May trumpet to the world. My heart's subdued   250
    Even to the very quality of my lord.
    I saw Othello's visage in his mind,
    And to his honours and his valiant parts
    Did I my soul and fortunes consecrate.
    So that, dear lords, if I be left behind,   255
    A moth of peace, and he go to the war,
    The rites for which I love him are bereft me,
    And I a heavy interim shall support
    By his dear absence. Let me go with him.

Othello: Let her have your voices.   260
    Vouch with me, heaven, I therefore beg it not

263	*heat:* sexual desire or drive
263–264	*the young ... defunct:* the passions of youth that I have now outlived
264	*and proper satisfaction:* the consummation of the marriage
265	*free and bounteous:* noble and generous; *to her mind:* The marriage is one of minds.
266	*heaven defend ... think:* Heaven forbid you good people (souls) from thinking that.
267	*scant:* neglect
268	*For:* because; *toys:* trifles, unimportant things
268	*feather'd Cupid:* Cupid is normally illustrated as an infant with wings—here the implication in "light-wing'd toys" is erotic pleasures. *seel:* blind (literally, sew up); *wanton:* lustful or lascivious
270	*My ... instruments:* my powers of sight and action
271	*That:* so that; *disports:* amusements
272	*helm:* helmet
273	*indign:* unworthy
274	*Make ... estimation:* form an army to attack and destroy my reputation
281	*commission:* formal appointment
282–283	*quality ... you:* of a type that concern you or have to do with you and your status
285	*conveyance:* transport, escort
289	*delighted:* delightful
292	*Look to:* watch, pay attention to. Iago will later make use of this warning (Act 3, Scene 3, line 206).

To please the palate of my appetite,
Nor to comply with heat—the young affects
In me defunct—and proper satisfaction;
But to be free and bounteous to her mind;   265
And heaven defend your good souls that you think
I will your serious and great business scant
For she is with me. No, when light-wing'd toys
Of feather'd Cupid seel with wanton dullness
My speculative and officed instruments,   270
That my disports corrupt and taint my business,
Let housewives make a skillet of my helm,
And all indign and base adversities
Make head against my estimation!
Duke: Be it as you shall privately determine,   275
  Either for her stay or going. The affair cries haste,
  And speed must answer it. You must hence to-night.
Desdemona: To-night, my lord?
Duke: This night.
Othello: With all my heart.
Duke: At nine i' the morning here we'll meet again.
  Othello, leave some officer behind,   280
  And he shall our commission bring to you,
  With such things else of quality and respect
  As doth import you.
Othello: So please your grace, my ancient;
  A man he is of honesty and trust.
  To his conveyance I assign my wife,   285
  With what else needful your good grace shall think
  To be sent after me.
Duke: Let it be so.
  Good night to every one. [*To Brabantio.*] And, noble signior,
  If virtue no delighted beauty lack,
  Your son-in-law is far more fair than black.   290
First Senator: Adieu, brave Moor. Use Desdemona well.
Brabantio: Look to her, Moor, if thou hast eyes to see:
  She has deceived her father, and may thee.
                  [*Exeunt Duke, Senators, Officers, and Attendants.*]

294   *My ... faith:* I would bet my life on her loyalty to me.

297   *in the best advantage:* at the best time

305   *incontinently:* immediately, at once

310–311   *four times seven years:* Iago is 28 years old.

314   *guinea hen:* Iago's term of contempt for Desdemona; *change:* exchange

316   *fond:* overly affectionate, foolishly in love

317   *virtue:* strength

318   *fig:* an obscene gesture using the thumb, and therefore a term of contempt

321   *hyssop:* a small bushy aromatic herb used medicinally; *gender:* species

322   *distract it with:* divide it among

324   *corrigible authority:* corrective power; *balance:* a type of scale

325   *poise:* weight against

326   *blood and baseness:* animal instincts. "Blood" refers to the passions.

328   *motions:* emotions; *carnal stings:* lustful desires

329   *unbitted:* uncontrolled, as in a horse without a bit

Othello: My life upon her faith! Honest Iago,
My Desdemona must I leave to thee. 295
I prithee, let thy wife attend on her,
And bring them after in the best advantage.
Come, Desdemona. I have but an hour
Of love, of worldly matters and direction,
To spend with thee. We must obey the time. 300

[*Exeunt Moor and Desdemona.*]

Roderigo: Iago!
Iago: What say'st thou, noble heart?
Roderigo: What will I do, thinkest thou?
Iago: Why, go to bed and sleep.
Roderigo: I will incontinently drown myself. 305
Iago: If thou dost, I shall never love thee after. Why, thou silly
gentleman?
Roderigo: It is silliness to live when to live is torment; and then
have we a prescription to die when death is our physician.
Iago: O villainous! I have looked upon the world for four times 310
seven years; and since I could distinguish betwixt a benefit
and an injury, I never found man that knew how to love
himself. Ere I would say I would drown myself for the love
of a guinea hen, I would change my humanity with
a baboon. 315
Roderigo: What should I do? I confess it is my shame to be so fond,
but it is not in my virtue to amend it.
Iago: Virtue? a fig! 'Tis in ourselves that we are thus or thus.
Our bodies are our gardens, to the which our wills are
gardeners; so that if we will plant nettles or sow lettuce, set 320
hyssop and weed up thyme, supply it with one gender of
herbs or distract it with many, either to have it sterile with
idleness or manured with industry, why, the power and
corrigible authority of this lies in our wills. If the balance of
our lives had not one scale of reason to poise another of 325
sensuality, the blood and baseness of our natures would
conduct us to most preposterous conclusions. But we have
reason to cool our raging motions, our carnal stings, our
unbitted lusts; whereof I take this that you call love to be a

330	*sect or scion:* cutting, offshoot. Love is a mere offshoot or byproduct of human lust.
335	*perdurable:* durable, lasting
336	*stead:* help
336–337	*Put money in thy purse:* an appeal to Roderigo to sell his land and material goods to obtain cash. (Note the number of times Iago makes his appeal in this exchange.)
338–339	*defeat ... beard:* grow a beard as a disguise
341–342	*answerable sequestration:* similar rupture or divorce; something equally violent
343	*wills:* desires
344	*locusts:* a sweet fruit like blackberries
345	*coloquintida:* a medical purgative derived from a bitter apple; *change for youth:* make an exchange for a younger man
348	*wilt needs:* must
349–350	*Make ... canst:* raise all the cash you can
350	*sanctimony:* the sacred vow of marriage; *an erring:* a wandering
353	*A pox of:* a plague on; forget about. Pox is a viral disease, and the word is frequently associated with syphilis.
353–354	*clean ... way:* totally beside the point
354	*compassing:* achieving
356	*fast:* constant, firm
357	*Thou ... me:* I am trustworthy
359	*hearted:* firmly in my heart; *be conjunctive:* closely united
360	*cuckold:* to deceive a husband by sleeping with his wife; a man who has been so deceived
362	*Traverse:* march

sect or scion. 330

Roderigo: It cannot be.

Iago: It is merely a lust of the blood and a permission of the will.
Come, be a man! Drown thyself? Drown cats and blind
puppies. I have professed me thy friend, and I confess me
knit to thy deserving with cables of perdurable toughness. 335
I could never better stead thee than now. Put money in
thy purse. Follow thou the wars; defeat thy favour with an
usurped beard. I say, put money in thy purse. It cannot be
that Desdemona should long continue her love to the
Moor—put money in thy purse—nor he his to her. It was a 340
violent commencement, and thou shalt see an answerable
sequestration—put but money in thy purse. These Moors
are changeable in their wills—fill thy purse with money. The
food that to him now is as luscious as locusts shall be to him
shortly as bitter as coloquintida. She must change for youth: 345
when she is sated with his body, she will find the error of
her choice. She must have change, she must. Therefore put
money in thy purse. If thou wilt needs damn thyself, do it a
more delicate way than drowning. Make all the money thou
canst. If sanctimony and a frail vow betwixt an erring 350
barbarian and a supersubtle Venetian be not too hard for
my wits and all the tribe of hell, thou shalt enjoy her.
Therefore make money. A pox of drowning thyself! It is clean
out of the way. Seek thou rather to be hanged in compassing
thy joy than to be drowned and go without her. 355

Roderigo: Wilt thou be fast to my hopes, if I depend on the issue?

Iago: Thou art sure of me. Go, make money. I have told thee often,
and I re-tell thee again and again, I hate the Moor. My cause
is hearted; thine hath no less reason. Let us be conjunctive
in our revenge against him. If thou canst cuckold him, thou 360
dost thyself a pleasure, me a sport. There are many events
in the womb of time, which will be delivered. Traverse, go,
provide thy money! We will have more of this to-morrow.
Adieu.

Roderigo: Where shall we meet i' the morning? 365

Iago: At my lodging.

367   *betimes:* early

368   *Go to:* roughly, "get on with it," an expression of impatience

373   *profane:* violate, pollute, misuse

374   *snipe:* a simple-minded person. A snipe is a woodcock, considered to be a stupid bird.

377   *my office:* my sexual duty as a husband

378   *in that kind:* in that regard

379   *as if for surety:* as if I were certain about it; *well:* in high regard

381   *proper:* appealing

382   *plume up my will:* to make myself more proud and please or satisfy my ego

385   *he:* Cassio; *his:* Othello's

386   *dispose:* disposition, manner

388   *free:* free from suspicion, *open:* sincere

389   *that but:* who only

390   *tenderly:* readily, willingly

392   *engender'd:* conceived

Roderigo: I'll be with thee betimes.

Iago: Go to, farewell. Do you hear, Roderigo?

Roderigo: What say you?

Iago: No more of drowning, do you hear? 370

Roderigo: I am changed. I'll go sell all my land. [*Exit.*]

Iago: Thus do I ever make my fool my purse;
    For I mine own gain'd knowledge should profane
    If I would time expend with such a snipe
    But for my sport and profit. I hate the Moor; 375
    And it is thought abroad that 'twixt my sheets
    He has done my office. I know not if't be true;
    Yet I, for mere suspicion in that kind,
    Will do as if for surety. He holds me well;
    The better shall my purpose work on him. 380
    Cassio's a proper man. Let me see now:
    To get his place, and to plume up my will
    In double knavery—How, how?—Let's see:—
    After some time, to abuse Othello's ear
    That he is too familiar with his wife. 385
    He hath a person and a smooth dispose
    To be suspected, framed to make women false.
    The Moor is of a free and open nature
    That thinks men honest that but seem to be so;
    And will as tenderly be led by the nose 390
    As asses are.
    I have't! It is engender'd! Hell and night
    Must bring this monstrous birth to the world's light. [*Exit.*]

Act 1, Scene 3: Activities

1. The possibility of a war with Turkey seems to pervade this part of the play. Research why Venice would want to keep a colony on Cyprus. The map on page ii will provide some sense of perspective. Why was Cyprus such an important island? Why would the Venetian government send its most respected general there to defend it against attack? You could report your findings to the class if you choose to do this activity in groups. What does the threat of war, which seems to hang over the whole play, contribute to the plot?

2. a) Court sessions are often pompous and formal events. Decide in your group how you would stage this scene. Describe the costumes the members of the senate, Brabantio, and Othello would wear if you were filming it.

   OR

   b) How would you, as a senator, deal with Brabantio's outrage? Why would he get away with making such a scene at all? Do you think his outrage is justified? How would you feel if you were Brabantio? What do you think he does after the court is dismissed? Imagine a dialogue between Brabantio and another senator after the court session is concluded.

3. In an essay, discuss whether or not the senators really do justice to Brabantio's charges against Othello. Does their quick dismissal of the charges prove that they are more concerned about the situation in Cyprus than they are about civil justice? It appears that they need a military man to solve their problems. How far will people go to get what they want? When does the necessity to act quickly take precedence over social law? Is the Duke right in his decision? Is Othello right in accepting what he is asked to do?

4. The session with the Duke raises the question, "What takes precedence, individual rights or the needs of the state?" Present your views on this issue in a carefully constructed magazine article.

5. In his soliloquy, Iago describes his plotting by using images of hunting and trapping. Make a list of these images and look back on the scenes you have read to see if there are any others that suggest the same thing. Update this list as the play progresses. When a person speaks in these terms, what might it suggest about his or her character? Note similar references that you recall from TV shows or movies you have seen. Listen carefully to conversations among your peers, and give an account of how many times you have heard people use such metaphors to describe situations. In an opinion piece for a newspaper, address your column to the issue of "predator and prey" as a familiar theme used to describe survival in society. (Sports are a good source for such metaphors.)

6. If Iago is indeed as devious as he appears to be, why is it that nobody else in the play figures him out? Perhaps he is just a "stock" dramatic figure. Or perhaps everyone else in the play is, to some degree, as devious as he is. Write an essay expressing your opinion on this issue.

7. In his soliloquy, Iago seems to confess everything to the audience by letting them in on his secret. Why does he do this—to gain sympathy? To show how clever or superior he is? To suggest how gullible everybody else is? To suggest that his method is the best one for survival? Or that such behaviour is just a form of "fun"? To best everyone else because he is the only person using "reason" to succeed? Because he is truly, and justifiably, a bitter person? Because he is misunderstood? Discuss this with your group, and create a profile of Iago when you have reached a decision. If you cannot reach a consensus, write an entry in your journal in which you assess his character. What do you think a psychiatrist would say about Iago's behaviour?

8. With your group, discuss why you think Roderigo is so ready to believe everything Iago says. How do you feel about Roderigo? Does he remind you of anyone you know? Does a person like Roderigo possess any of the public virtues that we are taught to value? What motivates him? Create a cartoon depicting Iago in conversation with Roderigo. Your caption should make your point of view absolutely clear.

9. People who show insolent contempt for others can be frightening. What is frightening about them? If you believe that Iago is such a person, what might you say to him in a conversation in which he expresses his views about humanity? Record your conversation for inclusion in an article you write for a magazine titled Great Villains of the World.

Act 1: Consider the Whole Act

1. Imagine you are a tour operator promoting a trip to Cyprus for Venetians at the time of the play. Create and design a travel brochure or folder that might make this destination attractive to prospective travellers. What attractions might you focus on— beaches, nightlife, tranquillity, history, architecture, culture, adventure? Given the unsettled circumstances between Turkey and Venice, what cautions might you pass on to your clients?

2. Design a poster that might appear in prominent public places in Venice announcing the war with Turkey. Since this is likely to be a form of subtle propaganda, be careful how you word your bulletin. How might you illustrate it without appearing unduly inflammatory?

3. There seems to be a sense among the Venetians in the play that they are in some way superior to everyone else. What sorts of things do they take great pride in? Historically, what did Venetians think about themselves in relation to the rest of the world? In your opinion, was there any justification for such an attitude? Some research will be required before you write a succinct essay on this topic.

4. There is not much of a plot to this play so far. How would you summarize the action to this point? If the plot isn't extensive, then what gives the play its momentum? You might want to discuss this with your group or with a partner before you write your own analysis.

5. Discuss with your group who you think is the driving force behind the action of the play so far. How did this come to be, and what appears to be the story's likely conclusion? Create a conversation with the person you have selected to determine what he or she hopes to achieve. You may present your conversation as an interview, as a first-person narrative, as a poem, as a dialogue, or even as a soliloquy.

For the next scene ...

Sometimes people tell lies deliberately to get what they want. Do you think that telling people what they want to hear is an effective way to win their affections? Have you ever used this strategy, and if you have, did it work? Why or why not?

Act 2, Scene 1

In this scene ...

On the island of Cyprus, Montano, the governor to be
replaced by Othello, awaits Othello's arrival anxiously
because a terrific storm has erupted. As a result, the
greater part of the attacking Turkish fleet is destroyed,
and while Othello's ship has been delayed, one carrying
Desdemona, Iago, Emilia and Roderigo, and another
bearing Cassio have arrived without incident. Cassio
tells Montano of Othello's marriage, and Desdemona
anxiously awaits the arrival of her husband. Iago and
Emilia exchange harsh words, and Desdemona defends
Emilia's character before chatting amicably with Cassio.
When Othello's ship arrives, the newlyweds express
their great happiness at their reunion. Iago, alone with
Roderigo, tells him that Desdemona is already tiring of
Othello and is now in love with Cassio, citing Desdemona
and Cassio's conversation as evidence. Iago persuades
Roderigo to help remove Cassio by annoying him in
some way so that Roderigo will be attacked. Iago will
then contrive to have Cassio dismissed from the
lieutenancy and removed as an obstacle to them both.
Roderigo agrees.

Stage Direction: *A sea-port in Cyprus*—likely Famagusta, which has an ancient castle nearby

2	*high-wrought flood:* heavy sea with great swells
3	*main:* open sea
7	*ruffian'd:* raged upon, attacked
8	*mountains:* enormous waves
9	*Can hold the mortise:* can hold their joints together. A mortise is a type of joint used in woodworking.
10	*segregation:* scattering, dispersing, breaking apart
12	*chidden billow:* the wave that appears to be driven by a wind, making a fearful noise: *chidden:* chiding, making an incessant noise
14–15	*Seems ... pole:* The constellation Ursa Minor (the Little Bear) contains two stars that are next in brightness to (guards to) the Polar (North) Star.
16	*like molestation:* similar turmoil, trouble, disturbance
17	*enchafed flood:* angry, furious sea
19	*bear it out:* can weather the storm
22	*designment halts:* plan is abandoned
23	*wreck:* disaster; *sufferance:* damage inflicted on

Act 2, Scene 1

A sea-port in Cyprus. An open place
near the quay.
Enter Montano and two Gentlemen.

Montano: What from the cape can you discern at sea?
First Gentleman: Nothing at all: it is a high-wrought flood.
    I cannot 'twixt the heaven and the main
    Descry a sail.
Montano: Methinks the wind hath spoke aloud at land;   5
    A fuller blast ne'er shook our battlements.
    If it hath ruffian'd so upon the sea,
    What ribs of oak, when mountains melt on them,
    Can hold the mortise? What shall we hear of this?
Second Gentleman: A segregation of the Turkish fleet;   10
    For do but stand upon the foaming shore,
    The chidden billow seems to pelt the clouds;
    The wind-shaked surge, with high and monstrous mane,
    Seems to cast water on the burning Bear
    And quench the Guards of the ever-fixed pole.   15
    I never did like molestation view
    On the enchafed flood.
Montano: If that the Turkish fleet
    Be not enshelter'd and embay'd, they are drown'd;
    It is impossible they bear it out.

    [*Enter a third Gentleman.*]

Third Gentleman: News, lads! Our wars are done.   20
    The desperate tempest hath so bang'd the Turks
    That their designment halts. A noble ship of Venice
    Hath seen a grievous wreck and sufferance
    On most part of their fleet.
Montano: How? Is this true?

25	*put in:* docked
26	*Veronesa:* out of Verona, then a tributary of the state of Venice, hence a "ship of Venice"; in Venetian service
29	*is ... commission:* comes with full powers
32	*Touching:* regarding, observing
36	*full:* perfect
39–40	*till ... regard:* until the sea and sky blend and become indistinguishable from one another
41–42	*every ... arrivance:* New arrivals are expected every minute.
48	*bark:* ship
49	*Of ... allowance:* considered to be expert and experienced
50	*surfeited to death:* overindulged or made ill by excess
51	*Stand in bold cure:* have hopes for a good recovery or success

Third Gentleman: The ship is here put in,   25
   A Veronesa; Michael Cassio,
   Lieutenant to the warlike Moor Othello,
   Is come on shore; the Moor himself at sea,
   And is in full commission here for Cyprus.
Montano: I am glad on't. 'Tis a worthy governor.   30
Third Gentleman: But this same Cassio, though he speak
     of comfort
   Touching the Turkish loss, yet he looks sadly
   And prays the Moor be safe, for they were parted
   With foul and violent tempest.
Montano: Pray heaven he be;
   For I have served him, and the man commands   35
   Like a full soldier. Let's to the seaside, ho!
   As well to see the vessel that's come in
   As to throw out our eyes for brave Othello,
   Even till we make the main and the aerial blue
   An indistinct regard.
Third Gentleman: Come, let's do so;   40
   For every minute is expectancy
   Of more arrivance.

   [*Enter Cassio.*]

Cassio: Thanks, you the valiant of this warlike isle,
   That so approve the Moor! O, let the heavens
   Give him defense against the elements,   45
   For I have lost him on a dangerous sea.
Montano: Is he well shipp'd?
Cassio: His bark is stoutly timber'd, and his pilot
   Of very expert and approved allowance;
   Therefore my hopes, not surfeited to death,   50
   Stand in bold cure.
            [*A cry within:* A sail, a sail, a sail!]

   [*Enter a fourth Gentleman.*]

Cassio: What noise?
Fourth Gentleman: The town is empty; on the brow o' the sea
   Stand ranks of people, and they cry "A sail!"

| 55 | *My hopes ... for:* I hope that it is, I imagine him to be |
| 56 | *shot of courtesy:* a friendly salute |

61	*achieved:* obtained or won
62	*paragons:* surpasses or excels
63	*quirks:* verbal wordplay, figures of speech; *blazoning:* boasting, describing
64–65	*in the ... ingener:* To describe the beauty God gave her exhausts the praiser.

| 67 | *happy:* fortunate, blessed |

69	*gutter'd:* jagged, grooved; *congregated sands:* sandbanks
70	*ensteep'd:* submerged; *clog:* obstruct
71	*As:* as if; *do omit:* refrain from
72	*mortal:* deadly

| 76 | *footing:* setting foot on land |
| 77 | *se'nnight's:* week's (seven-night's); *Jove:* Jupiter in Roman mythology, Zeus in Greek mythology |

| 81 | *extincted:* extinguished, dulled |

Cassio: My hopes do shape him for the governor.   55

                                        [*Guns heard.*]

Second Gentleman: They do discharge their shot of courtesy:
   Our friends at least.

Cassio: I pray you, sir, go forth
   And give us truth who 'tis that is arrived.

Second Gentleman: I shall.   [*Exit.*]

Montano: But, good lieutenant, is your general wived?   60

Cassio: Most fortunately. He hath achieved a maid
   That paragons description and wild fame;
   One that excels the quirks of blazoning pens,
   And in the essential vesture of creation
   Does tire the ingener.

[*Re-enter second Gentleman.*]

          How now? Who has put in?   65

Second Gentleman: 'Tis one Iago, ancient to the general.

Cassio: He has had most favourable and happy speed:
   Tempests themselves, high seas, and howling winds,
   The gutter'd rocks and congregated sands,
   Traitors ensteep'd to clog the guiltless keel,   70
   As having sense of beauty, do omit
   Their mortal natures, letting go safely by
   The divine Desdemona.

Montano: What is she?

Cassio: She that I spake of, our great captain's captain,
   Left in the conduct of the bold Iago,   75
   Whose footing here anticipates our thoughts
   A se'nnight's speed. Great Jove, Othello guard,
   And swell his sail with thine own powerful breath,
   That he may bless this bay with his tall ship,
   Make love's quick pants in Desdemona's arms,   80
   Give renew'd fire to our extincted spirits,
   And bring all Cyprus comfort!

[*Enter Desdemona, Iago, Roderigo, Emilia, and Attendants.*]

          O, behold,
The riches of the ship is come on shore!

84   *let ... knees:* kneel to her

87   *Enwheel thee round:* surround, encircle you

91   *How ... company:* What separated our ships and our company?

94   *their greeting:* their shot

98   *extend my manners:* extend my greeting to Emilia; *breeding:* nature (that leads me to this display of affectionate behaviour)

100   *would she ... her lips:* If she were to give you the same amount of her lips as she gives me her (sharp) tongue, you would have more than you want.

102   *she has no speech:* It appears she is not talkative.

104   *still:* always; *list:* wish

105   *Marry:* Mother Mary, an oath; *before:* in the presence of

107   *with thinking:* silently or quietly; only in her thoughts

109   *pictures ... doors:* pretty as pictures when you dress up to be seen in public

110   *Bells:* clanging bells

111   *Saints ... injuries:* When you are inclined to inflict injuries, you put on an appearance of innocence.

112   *housewifery:* one skilled in house management; *housewives:* hussies or loose women

Ye men of Cyprus, let her have your knees.
Hail to thee, lady! and the grace of heaven,   85
Before, behind thee, and on every hand,
Enwheel thee round!
Desdemona: I thank you, valiant Cassio.
What tidings can you tell me of my lord?
Cassio: He is not yet arrived; nor know I aught
But that he's well and will be shortly here.   90
Desdemona: O but I fear.—How lost you company?
Cassio: The great contention of the sea and skies
Parted our fellowship. But hark. A sail!
                    [*A cry within:* "A sail, a sail!" *Guns heard.*]
Second Gentleman: They give their greeting to the citadel;
This likewise is a friend.
Cassio: See for the news.   [*Exit Gentleman.*]   95
Good ancient, you are welcome. [*To Emilia.*] Welcome, mistress.
Let it not gall your patience, good Iago,
That I extend my manners. 'Tis my breeding
That gives me this bold show of courtesy.
                    [*Kissing her.*]
Iago: Sir, would she give you so much of her lips   100
As of her tongue she oft bestows on me,
You would have enough.
Desdemona: Alas, she has no speech!
Iago: In faith, too much.
I find it still when I have list to sleep.
Marry, before your ladyship, I grant,   105
She puts her tongue a little in her heart
And chides with thinking.
Emilia: You have little cause to say so.
Iago: Come on, come on. You are pictures out of doors,
Bells in your parlours, wildcats in your kitchens,   110
Saints in your injuries, devils being offended,
Players in your housewifery, and housewives in your beds.
Desdemona: O, fie upon thee, slanderer!
Iago: Nay, it is true, or else I am a Turk:
You rise to play, and go to bed to work.   115

116	*You shall not ..: praise:* I don't want you writing about my virtues if that is your attitude.
120	*assay:* try, put me to the test; *There's one gone:* has someone gone
122	*beguile:* disguise or divert attention from
123	*The thing I am:* the fact that I am anxious
125	*about it:* attempting to do it; *my invention:* inventiveness, creative ideas
126	*pate:* head; *birdlime:* a sticky paste spread on bushes to trap birds; *frieze:* a rough woollen cloth
127	*Muse:* The Muses were deities believed to inspire poets to write. *labours:* strains, works hard to give birth
128	*deliver'd:* gives birth
129	*fair:* light-complexioned, a sign of beauty; *wit:* intelligence, wisdom
130	*for use:* intended to be used
131	*black:* dark-haired or with a dark complexion; *witty:* clever, having sound judgement
133	*white:* a white man or "wight person"; the bull's-eye on a target. "To hit the white" means to hit the centre of the target. *fit:* possibly "hit"
137	*folly:* foolishness, playfulness, unpredictability, inconstancy
138	*fond:* foolish
140	*foul:* ugly
141	*thereunto:* besides
143	*heavy:* insightful, demanding deep study or thought
145–146	*one that ... itself:* one so worthy and deserving that even malice would be forced to approve of or stand up for her
147	*ever:* always
148	*tongue at will:* was never at a loss for the right words, knew the appropriate things to say
149	*gay:* elegantly or extravagantly dressed
150	*Fled ... may:* restrained herself from what she desired but knew when she could have what she wanted

Emilia: You shall not write my praise.

Iago: No, let me not.

Desdemona: What wouldst thou write of me, if thou shouldst
     praise me?

Iago: O gentle lady, do not put me to't,
     For I am nothing if not critical.

Desdemona: Come on, assay.—There's one gone to the harbour?   120

Iago: Ay, madam.

Desdemona: I am not merry; but I do beguile
     The thing I am by seeming otherwise.
     Come, how wouldst thou praise me?

Iago: I am about it; but indeed my invention   125
     Comes from my pate as birdlime does from frieze;
     It plucks out brains and all. But my Muse labours,
     And thus she is deliver'd:
     If she be fair and wise, fairness and wit,
     The one's for use, the other useth it.   130

Desdemona: Well praised! How if she be black and witty?

Iago: If she be black, and thereto have a wit,
     She'll find a white that shall her blackness fit.

Desdemona: Worse and worse.

Emilia: How if fair and foolish?   135

Iago: She never yet was foolish that was fair,
     For even her folly help'd her to an heir.

Desdemona: These are old fond paradoxes to make fools laugh i'
     the alehouse. What miserable praise hast thou for her that's
     foul and foolish?   140

Iago: There's none so foul, and foolish thereunto
     But does foul pranks which fair and wise ones do.

Desdemona: O heavy ignorance! Thou praisest the worst best. But
     what praise couldst thou bestow on a deserving woman
     indeed, one that in the authority of her merit did justly put   145
     on the vouch of very malice itself?

Iago: She that was ever fair, and never proud;
     Had tongue at will, and yet was never loud;
     Never lack'd gold, and yet went never gay;
     Fled from her wish, and yet said "Now I may";   150

152	*Bade ... fly:* suffered her wrongs (injuries) patiently and controlled her anger
154	*To ... tail:* exchange something valuable for something useless. "Head" and "tail" have additional obscene implications. The head was the best part of the cod, the tail the worst of the salmon.
157	*wight:* person
159	*suckle ... beer:* nurse babies and keep track of (chronicle) household trivialities
161	*of:* from; *How say you:* What do you have to say?
162	*profane;* irreverent, coarse; *liberal:* unrestrained, sexually promiscuous or deviant
163	*home:* to the point; *relish:* appreciate; *in:* in the role of
167–168	*gyve ... courtship:* shackle (bind) you with your own elegant (courtly) gestures (manners)
170	*kissed ... fingers:* a courtly gesture
171	*the sir:* fine gentleman
172	*curtsy:* courtesy
173	*clyster-pipes:* tubes inserted into the rectum to deliver enema medicine (clysters)
178	*warrior:* a term frequently used for women in love poetry; here, a term of endearment
184	*Olympus:* the highest mountain in Greece where the gods of Greek mythology lived

She that, being anger'd, her revenge being nigh,
Bade her wrong stay, and her displeasure fly;
She that in wisdom never was so frail
To change the cod's head for the salmon's tail;
She that could think, and ne'er disclose her mind;   155
See suitors following, and not look behind:
She was a wight, if ever such wight were—
Desdemona: To do what?
Iago: To suckle fools and chronicle small beer.
Desdemona: O most lame and impotent conclusion! Do not learn   160
    of him, Emilia, though he be thy husband. How say you,
    Cassio? Is he not a most profane and liberal counsellor?
Cassio: He speaks home, madam. You may relish him more in the
    soldier than in the scholar.
Iago: [*Aside.*] He takes her by the palm. Ay, well said, whisper!   165
    With as little a web as this will I ensnare as great a fly as
    Cassio. Ay, smile upon her, do! I will gyve thee in thine own
    courtship. You say true; 'tis so, indeed. If such tricks as these
    strip you out of your lieutenantry, it had been better you
    had not kissed your three fingers so oft, which now again   170
    you are most apt to play the sir in. Very good! well kissed!
    an excellent curtsy! 'Tis so, indeed. Yet again your fingers
    to your lips? Would they were clyster-pipes for your sake!
    [*Trumpet within.*] The Moor! I know his trumpet.
Cassio: 'Tis truly so.   175
Desdemona: Let's meet him and receive him.
Cassio: Lo, where he comes.

    [*Enter Othello and Attendants.*]

Othello: O my fair warrior!
Desdemona: My dear Othello!
Othello: It gives me wonder great as my content
    To see you here before me. O my soul's joy!   180
    If after every tempest come such calms,
    May the winds blow till they have waken'd death!
    And let the labouring bark climb hills of seas
    Olympus-high, and duck again as low

185	*if ... die:* if I were to die right now
187	*hath ... absolute:* my soul has discovered such total contentment
188	*comfort:* joy
189	*Succeeds:* follows; *unknown fate:* in the unforeseen future

| 193 | *here:* in my heart |

196	*set ... music:* ruin the harmony as if by loosening the pegs used to tune a stringed instrument
197	*As honest as I am:* for all my supposed honesty

| 200 | *well desired:* warmly welcomed |

202	*prattle ... fashion:* chatter on inappropriately (contrary to what is expected)
204	*disembark my coffers:* unload my trunks, as in luggage
205	*master:* captain or commander of a ship

| 207 | *challenge:* deserve |

| 211 | *base:* worthless |

213–214	*watches ... guard:* stands watch at the main guardhouse
214	*directly:* completely

As hell's from heaven! If it were now to die,   185
'Twere now to be most happy; for I fear
My soul hath her content so absolute
That not another comfort like to this
Succeeds in unknown fate.
Desdemona: The heavens forbid
But that our loves and comforts should increase   190
Even as our days do grow.
Othello: Amen to that, sweet powers!
I cannot speak enough of this content;
It stops me here; it is too much of joy.
And this, and this, the greatest discords be   [*Kissing her.*]
That e'er our hearts shall make!
Iago: [*Aside.*]   O, you are well tuned now!   195
But I'll set down the pegs that make this music,
As honest as I am.
Othello: Come, let us to the castle.
News, friends! Our wars are done; the Turks are drown'd.
How does my old acquaintance of this isle?
Honey, you shall be well desired in Cyprus;   200
I have found great love amongst them. O my sweet,
I prattle out of fashion, and I dote
In mine own comforts. I prithee, good Iago,
Go to the bay and disembark my coffers.
Bring thou the master to the citadel;   205
He is a good one, and his worthiness
Does challenge much respect. Come, Desdemona,
Once more well met at Cyprus.
                    [*Exeunt all but Iago and Roderigo.*]
Iago: [*To an Attendant, who goes out.*] Do thou meet me presently
    at the harbour. [*To Roderigo.*] Come hither. If thou be'st   210
    valiant—as they say base men being in love have then a
    nobility in their natures more than is native to them—list
    me. The lieutenant to-night watches on the court of
    guard. First, I must tell thee this: Desdemona is directly
    in love with him.   215
Roderigo: With him? Why, 'tis not possible.

217	*Lay ... thus:* lay your finger on your lips to stop them while you listen to a wiser man; *Mark me:* pay attention to
218	*but:* only
219	*still:* always
220	*prating:* chattering, talking foolishly
221	*the devil:* Othello, because devils were thought to be black
222	*blood:* sexual drive; *act of sport:* sexual intercourse
224	*favour:* attractiveness, looks; *sympathy in years:* similarity in age
226	*conveniences:* advantages, comforts
227	*heave the gorge:* vomit; *disrelish:* dislike (the taste of)
228	*Very nature:* her natural instincts
230	*pregnant ... position:* obvious and natural or likely argument
230–231	*stands ... fortune as:* is most probable to benefit from this as
232	*conscionable:* ruled by conscience
233	*humane seeming:* polite and courteous appearance, highly regarded
234	*compassing:* embracing; *salt:* lecherous, lustful
235	*slipper:* slippery
236–237	*stamp ... advantages:* make false or fraudulent opportunities
239	*green:* young, inexperienced
240	*look after:* search for; *pestilent:* poisonous
243	*condition:* disposition, character
244	*Blessed fig's-end:* an obscene oath and gesture that was accomplished by thrusting the thumb between two of the closed fingers or into the mouth; thus, an expression of contempt; *wine ... grapes:* roughly, she is no different from the rest of us
246	*Blessed pudding:* an oath of contempt. A pudding is a term for a sausage, so the oath is obscene. *paddle with:* fondle or play with the fingers upon
247	*his:* meaning Cassio's
249–250	*index ... history:* the material preceding the real story or introduction. Indexes were formerly prefixed to books.
252	*mutualities:* familiarities, exchange of intimacies
252–253	*marshal the way:* point out the way
253	*hard to hand:* immediately, close at hand; *master and main exercise:* principal exercise or action, also sexual

Iago: Lay thy finger thus, and let thy soul be instructed. Mark me
with what violence she first loved the Moor, but for bragging
and telling her fantastical lies; and will she love him still for
prating? Let not thy discreet heart think it. Her eye must be   220
fed; and what delight shall she have to look on the devil?
When the blood is made dull with the act of sport, there
should be, again to inflame it and to give satiety a fresh
appetite, loveliness in favour, sympathy in years, manners,
and beauties; all which the Moor is defective in. Now for   225
want of these required conveniences, her delicate tenderness
will find itself abused, begin to heave the gorge, disrelish
and abhor the Moor. Very nature will instruct her in it and
compel her to some second choice. Now, sir, this granted—as
it is a most pregnant and unforced position—who stands so   230
eminent in the degree of this fortune as Cassio does? A
knave very voluble; no further conscionable than in putting
on the mere form of civil and humane seeming for the better
compassing of his salt and most hidden loose affection?
Why, none! why, none! A slipper and subtle knave; a finder-   235
out of occasions; that has an eye can stamp and counterfeit
advantages, though true advantage never present itself; a
devilish knave! Besides, the knave is handsome, young, and
hath all those requisites in him that folly and green minds
look after. A pestilent complete knave! and the woman hath   240
found him already.

Roderigo: I cannot believe that in her; she's full of most blessed
condition.

Iago: Blessed fig's-end! The wine she drinks is made of grapes.
If she had been blessed, she would never have loved the   245
Moor. Blessed pudding! Didst thou not see her paddle with
the palm of his hand? Didst not mark that?

Roderigo: Yes, that I did; but that was but courtesy.

Iago: Lechery, by this hand! an index and obscure prologue to the
history of lust and foul thoughts. They met so near with   250
their lips that their breaths embraced together. Villainous
thoughts, Roderigo! When these mutualities so marshal the
way, hard at hand comes the master and main exercise, the

254	*incorporate:* united in one body; the sexual act; *Pish:* expression of disgust, contempt, or annoyance
255	*Watch you:* take or stand the watch
256	*command:* your orders to be a part of the watch
258	*tainting:* disparaging
260	*minister:* supply, provide
262	*sudden in choler:* suddenly aroused to anger; *haply:* perhaps
264	*mutiny:* riot
264–266	*whose ... of Cassio:* Cypriots who will not be satisfied except by Cassio's dismissal from service
267	*prefer:* promote
268	*impediment:* an obvious reference to Cassio
270	*bring ... opportunity:* arrange an opportunity
275	*apt ... credit:* fitting and quite believable
276	*howbeit:* however it may be
280	*absolute:* pure and simple
281	*accountant:* responsible
282	*diet:* feed, the implication being that revenge needs to be fed
283	*For that:* because
285	*inwards:* inward parts, "innards," "guts"
288	*yet that:* until I am able to
290	*judgement:* reason (Othello's)

incorporate conclusion. Pish! But, sir, be you ruled by me:
I have brought you from Venice. Watch you to-night;   255
for the command, I'll lay't upon you. Cassio knows you
not. I'll not be far from you: do you find some occasion to
anger Cassio, either by speaking too loud, or tainting his
discipline, or from what other course you please which the
time shall more favourably minister.   260

Roderigo: Well.

Iago: Sir, he is rash and very sudden in choler, and haply may
strike at you. Provoke him that he may; for even out of that
will I cause these of Cyprus to mutiny; whose qualification
shall come into no true taste again but by the displanting of 265
Cassio. So shall you have a shorter journey to your desires
by the means I shall then have to prefer them; and the
impediment most profitably removed, without the which
there were no expectation of our prosperity.

Roderigo: I will do this if you can bring it to any opportunity.   270

Iago: I warrant thee. Meet me by and by at the citadel;
I must fetch his necessaries ashore. Farewell.

Roderigo: Adieu.   [*Exit.*]

Iago: That Cassio loves her, I do well believe it;
That she loves him, 'tis apt and of great credit.   275
The Moor, howbeit that I endure him not,
Is of a constant, loving, noble nature,
And I dare think he'll prove to Desdemona
A most dear husband. Now I do love her too;
Not out of absolute lust, though peradventure   280
I stand accountant for as great a sin,
But partly led to diet my revenge,
For that I do suspect the lusty Moor
Hath leap'd into my seat; the thought whereof
Doth, like a poisonous mineral, gnaw my inwards;   285
And nothing can or shall content my soul
Till I am even'd with him, wife for wife;
Or failing so, yet that I put the Moor
At least into a jealousy so strong
That judgement cannot cure. Which thing to do,   290

291–292 *If … on:* If I can prevent this worthless human being from hunting too fast and blindly, I can make him hunt more quickly with more focus and more productively in the direction I want.

293 *I'll … hip:* I will have Cassio in a winning hold. "On the hip" is a wrestling term meaning to have an opponent at a disadvantage.

294 *Abuse:* slander, misrepresent; *rank garb:* make him appear lustful (dress him in implicating clothes to make him appear to be having an affair with Desdemona)

295 *For I fear … too:* Possibly Iago is claiming that Cassio has slept with Emilia, as well.

297 *egregiously:* conspicuously, obviously, blatantly

298 *practising upon:* plotting against

299–300 *'Tis … used:* My plan is there, though not yet clearly developed in my head, and it won't really materialize until the opportunity suggests that it is time for it to be implemented.

If this poor trash of Venice, whom I trash
For his quick hunting, stand the putting on,
I'll have our Michael Cassio on the hip,
Abuse him to the Moor in the rank garb—
For I fear Cassio with my nightcap too—   295
Make the Moor thank me, love me, and reward me
For making him egregiously an ass
And practising upon his peace and quiet
Even to madness. 'Tis here, but yet confused:
Knavery's plain face is never seen till used.   [*Exit.*]   300

Act 2, Scene 1: Activities

1. The storm that opens this scene suggests many things thematically. With your group, make a list of the things this scene suggests to you. What makes this an effective beginning for what is essentially Part Two of the play? The external threat of a Turkish return is never mentioned again—why do you suppose this is? In your opinion, what is the purpose of this glimpse of turmoil, confusion, and uncertainty in the external world?

2. It doesn't take Iago long to pick up where he left off. Refer again to his soliloquy in Act 1, Scene 3, and then note his responses to Cassio, Desdemona, and his own wife, Emilia, in this scene (lines 100–175). What more can we determine about Iago and his views about other people from his comments? What seems to motivate him if not loyalty? Update the character sketch of Iago you started in Act 1, quoting appropriate lines that might give further insights into what kind of an individual he is. How do you feel about him now?

3. Iago's second soliloquy (lines 274–300) reveals more information about him. State in your own words what he is saying here. Rehearse this speech and deliver it either to your group or to the class. You might choose to present this as a dramatic reading of the script so that you don't have to memorize the speech. Decide what impression you are trying to convey. What words and lines will you emphasize? Consider what you think is the most important line in this speech. What movements might you incorporate? What tone of voice will you use? As Iago, are you amused, pleased with your handiwork so far, or just nasty?

4. Iago obviously doesn't care at all about Roderigo. He does, though, seem to care about Roderigo's money. Do you think Iago really wants only Roderigo's wealth, or does he have some other motive? Discuss this situation with your group and decide what is really going on here.

5. You may be familiar with Virgil's quotation "Love conquers all things; let us too surrender to Love." More often heard is its

abbreviated form, "Love conquers all." Discuss whether or not you think Othello believes this. Does Iago? What is your personal opinion? In your journal, record what the consequences might be if Virgil's statement is followed blindly. Create a quotation of your own to reflect your view of love as it appears so far in this play.

6. Look up the word "jealousy" in a dictionary. Discuss with your group what *you* think the word means. Draw a picture of it. The play demonstrates that jealousy can be a dangerous motivator. Why do you think Roderigo is so consumed by it? Iago sees jealousy as a tool to be used against people. How does he manage to do that? What are your own views on jealousy? In your journal, write about an incident in which jealousy led to unpleasant consequences. Do you view jealousy as a character flaw or just a normal part of human nature?

For the next scene ...

The words "party" or "festival" are used loosely to describe just about any celebration. Why do people hold parties? Is there a code of behaviour expected at these events? If so, what is it? What happens if the code is broken? What happens if nobody pays any attention to the unwritten rules?

Act 2, Scene 2

In this scene ...

A proclamation is read by a herald to the crowd indicating that Othello has decreed a night of celebration to mark the defeat of the Turkish fleet and to honour his marriage. The feasting is to take place from five o'clock until eleven o'clock that night.

2	*importing:* communicating, making known
2–3	*mere perdition:* total destruction
3–4	*put ... triumph:* join in the public celebration
5	*addiction:* inclination
7	*offices:* kitchens (and storerooms), which supplied food and beverages
9	*have told:* has proclaimed, tolled, struck

Scene 2

A street.
Enter Othello's Herald, with a
proclamation.

Herald: It is Othello's pleasure, our noble and valiant general, that
upon certain tidings now arrived, importing the mere
perdition of the Turkish fleet, every man put himself into
triumph; some to dance, some to make bonfires, each man to
what sport and revels his addiction leads him. For, besides   5
these beneficial news, it is the celebration of his nuptial. So
much was his pleasure should be proclaimed. All offices are
open, and there is full liberty of feasting from this present
hour of five till the bell have told eleven. Heaven bless the
isle of Cyprus and our noble general Othello!   [*Exit.*]   10

Act 2, Scene 2: Activities

1. Othello knows nothing about Cyprus, yet he declares a general party. With your group, discuss how wise you think such a move is.

2. We have all seen or heard about parties that got out of hand. What causes this to happen? Do you think such things are predictable? Why or why not? If you could talk to Othello before he made this decree, what advice would you offer him? Do you think Othello even thought about the dangers of a large, uncontrolled event, or do you think, as a military man, he was himself accustomed to such things?

For the next scene ...

Images reflect the way we see the world and people at any given time. Write down some images that immediately come to mind to describe a character in the play whom you either really like or really dislike. Look at what you have written, and create one definitive sentence that would sum up your current impressions of this person. Opinions change. What makes them change?

Act 2, Scene 3

In this scene ...

That evening, Iago convinces Cassio that they should share a container of wine with some Cypriots who want to toast Othello's health, even though Cassio knows he has had enough to drink already. Cassio quickly becomes quite drunk, and when he leaves, Iago remarks about Cassio's condition to Montano, who becomes quite concerned that Othello's lieutenant should have a drinking problem. Montano feels the general should be informed of this, but suddenly Cassio re-enters, chasing Roderigo, whom he then attacks violently. Montano intervenes, and Cassio attacks and wounds him. Aroused by all the noise, Othello arrives and commands the brawlers to stop. Othello is clearly upset by the quarrel and demands to know how it began. Iago relates the event, apparently reluctantly. He embellishes his version, implicating Cassio as the instigator. Trusting Iago, Othello feels forced to relieve Cassio of his commission as his lieutenant. Cassio is devastated by this sudden change of fortune, and Iago advises him that the best way to change Othello's mind is by getting Desdemona's help. Alone, Iago describes the next step in his plan, which is to turn Desdemona's "virtue into pitch." Through his wife, Emilia, he plans to arrange a meeting between Cassio and Desdemona and then to contrive to have Othello come upon Cassio pleading with Desdemona so that he, Iago, can convince Othello that the two are secretly lovers.

2   *Let's ... stop:* show restraint

3   *outsport discretion:* not to carry revelling beyond the limits of good taste or behaviour

7   *with your earliest:* at your earliest convenience

9   *purchase:* something acquired; *fruits:* indicating that the marriage has not yet been consummated. "Fruit" is a reference to children.

13   *Not this hour:* not for an hour

14   *cast:* disposed of, dismissed

16   *is ... Jove:* likely Jupiter, king of the Roman gods, who was a notorious womanizer and known for his sexual exploits with many mortal women. Iago implies that Desdemona is delectable enough to attract the desires of the gods.

18   *game:* sport; here, love-play

19   *fresh:* youthful, in prime condition (referring to women)

20–21   *sounds ... provocation:* A "parley" is literally a trumpet call announcing a meeting between opposing forces before a battle. The idea of the battle was often used metaphorically to mean sexual (or love) encounters; "provocation" means challenge in the same sense.

22   *right:* properly or very

23   *alarum:* a call to battle

Scene 3

A hall in the castle.
Enter Othello, Desdemona, Cassio,
and Attendants.

Othello: Good Michael, look you to the guard to-night.
  Let's teach ourselves that honourable stop,
  Not to outsport discretion.
Cassio: Iago hath direction what to do;
  But notwithstanding, with my personal eye   5
  Will I look to't.
Othello: Iago is most honest.
  Michael, good night. To-morrow with your earliest
  Let me have speech with you. Come, my dear love,
  The purchase made, the fruits are to ensue;
  That profit's yet to come 'tween me and you.   10
  Good night.
          [Exeunt Othello, Desdemona, and Attendants.]

[Enter Iago.]

Cassio: Welcome, Iago. We must to the watch.
Iago: Not this hour, lieutenant; 'tis not yet ten o' the clock. Our
    general cast us thus early for the love of his Desdemona; who
    let us not therefore blame. He hath not yet made wanton the 15
    night with her, and she is sport for Jove.
Cassio: She's a most exquisite lady.
Iago: And, I'll warrant her, full of game.
Cassio: Indeed, she's a most fresh and delicate creature.
Iago: What an eye she has! Methinks it sounds a parley to   20
    provocation.
Cassio: An inviting eye; and yet methinks right modest.
Iago: And when she speaks, is it not an alarum to love?
Cassio: She is indeed perfection.
Iago: Well, happiness to their sheets! Come, lieutenant, I have a 25

26	*stoup:* a tankard or container for wine, a drinking vessel (size varied); *brace:* two, or a pair
27	*fain ... measure:* that is, drink a quantity (of wine) as a toast or "health" to. "Fain" means gladly; "measure" means liquid measure.
29	*unhappy:* ill-suited
33–34	*craftily qualified:* skillfully diluted
34	*innovation:* change; *here:* that is, in his head
35	*task:* test or challenge
40	*dislikes:* I am not pleased (about it).
43	*be ... offence:* will show aggression toward, take offence
44	*my ... dog:* as any young woman's small (and presumably spoiled) dog, which can be quite aggressive and unpleasant
46	*caroused:* drunk many times
47	*Potations pottle-deep:* to the bottom of a large tankard (drinking vessel or cup); that is, he has consumed a lot of alcohol. A "pottle" is a small pot.
48	*lads:* other people; *swelling:* inflated with pride (proud of themselves)
49	*That ... distance:* who are quick to fight if they feel their honour is threatened
50	*The very elements:* the true specimens
51	*fluster'd:* confused (from drink)
55	*If ... dream:* if what follows confirms my hopes, or, more literally, if the result of this proves my dream true
57	*rouse:* carouse or, more literally, a long, deep drink
60	*canakin:* a little can used for drinking; *clink:* that is, to clink the can against someone else's, as in a toast

stoup of wine, and here without are a brace of Cyprus
gallants that would fain have a measure to the health of black
Othello.

Cassio: Not to-night, good Iago. I have very poor and unhappy
brains for drinking; I could well wish courtesy would invent 30
some other custom of entertainment.

Iago: O, they are our friends. But one cup! I'll drink for you.

Cassio: I have drunk but one cup to-night, and that was craftily
qualified too; and behold what innovation it makes here.
I am unfortunate in the infirmity and dare not task my 35
weakness with any more.

Iago: What, man! 'Tis a night of revels: the gallants desire it.

Cassio: Where are they?

Iago: Here at the door; I pray you call them in.

Cassio: I'll do't, but it dislikes me.   [*Exit.*] 40

Iago: If I can fasten but one cup upon him
With that which he hath drunk to-night already,
He'll be as full of quarrel and offence
As my young mistress' dog. Now my sick fool Roderigo,
Whom love hath turn'd almost the wrong side out, 45
To Desdemona hath to-night caroused
Potations pottle-deep; and he's to watch.
Three lads of Cyprus, noble swelling spirits,
That hold their honours in a wary distance,
The very elements of this warlike isle, 50
Have I to-night fluster'd with flowing cups,
And they watch too. Now, 'mongst this flock of drunkards
Am I to put our Cassio in some action
That may offend the isle. But here they come.
If consequence do but approve my dream, 55
My boat sails freely, both with wind and stream.

[*Re-enter Cassio; with him Montano and Gentlemen; Servants
following with wine.*]

Cassio: 'Fore God, they have given me a rouse already.

Montano: Good faith, a little one; not past a pint, as I am a soldier.

Iago: Some wine, ho!
[*Sings.*] *And let me the canakin clink, clink;* 60

63	*span:* a short time
67–68	*potent in potting:* heavy drinkers. Successful drinking among men was considered to be a sign of masculinity.
68	*swag-bellied:* having a prominent abdomen that hangs down and sways from side to side; pot-bellied
71–72	*he ... Alamain:* he can out-drink a German anytime
72–73	*gives ... vomit:* drinks enough to make a Dutchman throw up
75	*I'll ... justice:* drink the same amount as you do
77–84	*King Stephen ... thee:* a common and well-known song called "Bell My Wife," kind of a "filler" in a typical ballad, much like the chorus in a contemporary song; *lown:* lout, rogue
86	*exquisite:* accomplished
88	*place:* rank, position
93	*quality:* again, social standing

> *And let me the canakin clink.*
> *A soldier's a man;*
> *A life's but a span,*
> *Why then, let a soldier drink.*

Some wine, boys! 65

Cassio: 'Fore God, an excellent song!

Iago: I learned it in England, where indeed they are most potent in potting. Your Dane, your German, and your swag-bellied Hollander—Drink, ho!—are nothing to your English.

Cassio: Is your Englishman so expert in his drinking? 70

Iago: Why, he drinks you with facility your Dane dead drunk; he sweats not to overthrow your Almain; he gives your Hollander a vomit ere the next pottle can be filled.

Cassio: To the health of our general!

Montano: I am for it, lieutenant, and I'll do you justice. 75

Iago: O sweet England!

> [*Sings.*] *King Stephen was a worthy peer;*
> *His breeches cost him but a crown;*
> *He held 'em sixpence all too dear,*
> *With that he call'd the tailor lown.* 80
> *He was a wight of high renown,*
> *And thou art but of low degree.*
> *'Tis pride that pulls the country down;*
> *Then take thine auld cloak about thee.*

Some wine, ho! 85

Cassio: Why, this is a more exquisite song than the other.

Iago: Will you hear't again?

Cassio: No, for I hold him to be unworthy of his place that does those things. Well, God's above all; and there be souls must be saved, and there be souls must not be saved. 90

Iago: It's true, good lieutenant.

Cassio: For mine own part—no offence to the general, nor any man of quality—I hope to be saved.

Iago: And so do I too, lieutenant.

Cassio: Ay, but, by your leave, not before me. The lieutenant is to 95 be saved before the ancient. Let's have no more of this; let's to our affairs. God forgive us our sins! Gentlemen, let's look

104   *platform:* ramparts, or possibly a gun-platform

108   *just equinox:* a reference to the two days per year that have equal (balanced) hours of day and night. "Equinox" means "the same thing" or "the equivalent"; Cassio's supposed vice matches his virtue.

111   *On ... infirmity:* at a time when he is at his weakest point

114–115   *watch ... cradle:* He will stay awake for two complete rotations of the clock if drink doesn't lull him to sleep as if he were rocked in a cradle, or if he doesn't drink himself to sleep. The meaning is unclear.

124   *ingraft:* ingrained, deep-rooted

to our business. Do not think, gentlemen, I am drunk. This is
my ancient; this is my right hand, and this is my left. I am not
drunk now. I can stand well enough, and speak well enough. 100
All: Excellent well.
Cassio: Why, very well then. You must not think then that I am
    drunk.   [*Exit.*]
Montano: To the platform, masters. Come, let's set the watch.
Iago: You see this fellow that is gone before.   105
  He is a soldier fit to stand by Caesar
  And give direction; and do but see his vice.
  'Tis to his virtue a just equinox,
  The one as long as the other. 'Tis pity of him.
  I fear the trust Othello puts him in,   110
  On some odd time of his infirmity,
  Will shake this island.
Montano: But is he often thus?
Iago: 'Tis evermore the prologue to his sleep:
  He'll watch the horologe a double set
  If drink rock not his cradle.
Montano: It were well   115
  The general were put in mind of it.
  Perhaps he sees it not, or his good nature
  Prizes the virtue that appears in Cassio
  And looks not on his evils. Is not this true?

  [*Enter Roderigo.*]

Iago: [*Aside to him.*] How now, Roderigo?   120
  I pray you after the lieutenant, go!   [*Exit Roderigo.*]
Montano: And 'tis great pity that the noble Moor
  Should hazard such a place as his own second
  With one of an ingraft infirmity.
  It were an honest action to say   125
  So to the Moor.
Iago: Not I, for this fair island.
  I do love Cassio well and would do much
  To cure him of this evil.   [*A cry within:* "Help! help!"]
               But hark! What noise?

131   *twiggen bottle:* "Twiggen" means made of wicker or twigs woven together and often wrapped around wine bottles, so the implication is that the pattern of welts on his body will resemble this wicker structure or pattern.

133   *hold your hand:* do not strike (him)

134   *mazzard:* head, also cup

136   *cry a mutiny:* raise the cry of "riot"

140   *bell:* an alarm bell; *Diablo:* the devil

144   *Hold:* stop

149–150   *to ourselves ... Ottomites:* bring the same destruction down on ourselves that providence (heaven) has prevented the Turkish fleet from doing to us

151   *put by:* give up, cease

152   *to ... rage:* to carve (cut) for his own anger, to indulge his own rage

153   *Holds his soul light:* regards his soul as of small value; *upon his motion:* with his first move

[*Re-enter Cassio, driving in Roderigo.*]

Cassio: 'Zounds, you rogue! you rascal!

Montano: What's the matter, lieutenant?

Cassio: A knave teach me my duty? 130
  I'll beat the knave into a twiggen bottle.

Roderigo: Beat me?

Cassio: Dost thou prate, rogue?   [*Striking Roderigo.*]

Montano: Nay, good lieutenant!
                                    [*Staying him.*]
  I pray you, sir, hold your hand.

Cassio: Let me go, sir,
  Or I'll knock you o'er the mazzard.

Montano: Come, come, you're drunk!

Cassio: Drunk?   [*They fight.*]   135

Iago: [*Aside to Roderigo.*] Away, I say! Go out and cry a mutiny!
                               [*Exit Roderigo.*]
  Nay, good lieutenant. God's will, gentlemen!
  Help, ho!—lieutenant—sir—Montano—sir—
  Help, masters!—Here's a goodly watch indeed!
                              [*A bell rings.*]
  Who's that which rings the bell? Diablo, ho!   140
  The town will rise. God's will, lieutenant, hold!
  You will be shamed for ever.

[*Re-enter Othello and Attendants.*]

Othello: What is the matter here?

Montano: 'Zounds, I bleed still. I am hurt to the death.   [*Faints.*]

Othello: Hold for your lives!

Iago: Hold, ho! Lieutenant—sir—Montano—gentlemen!   145
  Have you forgot all sense of place and duty?
  Hold! The general speaks to you. Hold, hold, for shame!

Othello: Why, how now, ho? From whence ariseth this?
  Are we turn'd Turks, and to ourselves do that
  Which heaven hath forbid the Ottomites?   150
  For Christian shame put by this barbarous brawl!
  He that stirs next to carve for his own rage
  Holds his soul light; he dies upon his motion.

155	*From her propriety:* out of herself, out of her own nature or character
157	*On ... thee:* in the name of your love for me, I order you to speak
159	*In quarter ... terms:* in peace; relating peacefully (or lovingly) to others; "terms" means language
160	*Devesting them:* undressing themselves
161	*As if ... men:* as if the influence of a planet had driven them mad. Planets too close to Earth were thought to drive men mad.
162	*tilting ... breast:* thrusting at each other's chest
164	*peevish odds:* senseless quarrel
165	*would:* I wish I had
167	*you ... forgot:* have so forgotten yourself
169	*were ... civil:* you used to be civilized
170	*stillness:* quiet conduct
171	*name:* reputation (his name was greatly praised)
172	*censure:* judgement
173	*unlace:* undo (as in slicing open an animal's stomach to gut it)
174	*spend ... opinion:* waste or ruin your fine reputation
176	*hurt to danger:* seriously injured
178	*something ... me:* which somewhat hurts me. (My wounds make it difficult to speak.)
180	*By me ... amiss:* that I said or did anything wrong
181	*self-charity:* looking out for oneself
184	*My blood ... rule:* my anger or passion (blood) is overcoming my reason or judgement
185	*collied:* blackened
186	*Assays:* tries
189	*rout:* brawl, commotion

Silence that dreadful bell! It frights the isle
From her propriety. What is the matter, masters?   155
Honest Iago, that looks dead with grieving,
Speak. Who began this? On thy love, I charge thee.
Iago: I do not know. Friends all but now, even now,
   In quarter, and in terms like bride and groom
   Devesting them for bed; and then, but now—   160
   As if some planet had unwitted men—
   Swords out, and tilting one at other's breast
   In opposition bloody. I cannot speak
   Any beginning to this peevish odds,
   And would in action glorious I had lost   165
   Those legs that brought me to a part of it!
Othello: How comes it, Michael, you are thus forgot?
Cassio: I pray you pardon me; I cannot speak.
Othello: Worthy Montano, you were wont be civil;
   The gravity and stillness of your youth   170
   The world hath noted, and your name is great
   In mouths of wisest censure. What's the matter
   That you unlace your reputation thus
   And spend your rich opinion for the name
   Of a night-brawler? Give me answer to it.   175
Montano: Worthy Othello, I am hurt to danger.
   Your officer, Iago, can inform you—
   While I spare speech, which something now offends me—
   Of all that I do know; nor know I aught
   By me that's said or done amiss this night,   180
   Unless self-charity be sometimes a vice,
   And to defend ourselves it be a sin
   When violence assails us.
Othello: Now, by heaven,
   My blood begins my safer guides to rule,
   And passion, having my best judgement collied,   185
   Assays to lead the way. If I once stir
   Or do but lift this arm, the best of you
   Shall sink in my rebuke. Give me to know
   How this foul rout began, who set it on;

190	*approved:* proved guilty

192	*lose me:* lose my favour
193	*Yet:* still
194	*manage:* conduct, engage in
195	*on the ... safety:* and on the courtyard during guard duty protecting our general safety
197	*If ... office:* if bound to Cassio by partiality or because he is a colleague (fellow officer)

| 199 | *Touch me not so near:* It is unnecessary to make reference to (to take me to task for) something that concerns me as closely as my soldiering ability. |
| 201 | *offence:* harm |

| 207 | *To execute upon him:* to use against him, to express his anger against, perhaps even to harm or kill |

| 210 | *fell out:* happened |

| 212 | *the rather:* all the more quickly, sooner |
| 213 | *For that:* for that reason, because |

| 217 | *even:* just |

| 221 | *him:* Montano |

| 224 | *strange indignity:* unusual insult |
| 225 | *pass:* allow to (let) pass |

And he that is approved in this offence, 190
Though he had twinn'd with me, both at a birth,
Shall lose me. What! in a town of war,
Yet wild, the people's hearts brimful of fear,
To manage private and domestic quarrel?
In night, and on the court and guard of safety? 195
'Tis monstrous. Iago, who began't?
Montano: If partially affined, or leagued in office,
Thou dost deliver more or less than truth,
Thou art no soldier.
Iago: Touch me not so near.
I had rather have this tongue cut from my mouth 200
Than it should do offence to Michael Cassio;
Yet, I persuade myself, to speak the truth
Shall nothing wrong him. Thus it is, general.
Montano and myself being in speech,
There comes a fellow crying out for help, 205
And Cassio following him with determined sword
To execute upon him. Sir, this gentleman
Steps in to Cassio and entreats his pause.
Myself the crying fellow did pursue,
Lest by his clamour—as it so fell out— 210
The town might fall in fright. He, swift of foot,
Outran my purpose; and I return'd the rather
For that I heard the clink and fall of swords,
And Cassio high in oath; which till to-night
I ne'er might say before. When I came back— 215
For this was brief—I found them close together
At blow and thrust, even as again they were
When you yourself did part them.
More of this matter cannot I report;
But men are men; the best sometimes forget. 220
Though Cassio did some little wrong to him,
As men in rage strike those that wish them best,
Yet surely Cassio, I believe, received
From him that fled some strange indignity,
Which patience could not pass.

226   *mince:* diminish, make light of (for Cassio's benefit)

231   *sweeting:* sweetheart

240   *Marry:* an expression of surprise or indignation such as "indeed"

246   *imposition:* quality imposed on us by others

249   *recover:* regain (the favour of)
250   *cast ... mood:* dismissed because of his anger
250–251 *punishment ... malice:* punishment based on political reasons and not out of personal malice toward you
251–252 *even so ... lion:* just as to punish a man in the presence of, and for an example to, the powerful; that is, to frighten the strong. "Lion," likely refers to the Venetian army but is also a reference to the proverb "Beat the dog before the lion." Othello needs authority over both Venetians and Cypriots.
252   *Sue to:* petition him (for a pardon)
256   *speak parrot:* talk without sense, babble
257   *discourse fustian:* talk nonsense

Othello: I know, Iago,   225
  Thy honesty and love doth mince this matter,
  Making it light to Cassio. Cassio, I love thee;
  But never more be officer of mine.

  [*Enter Desdemona, attended.*]

  Look if my gentle love be not raised up!
  I'll make thee an example.
Desdemona: What's the matter?   230
Othello: All's well now, sweeting; come away to bed.
  [*To Montano.*] Sir, for your hurts, myself will be your surgeon.
  Lead him off.   [*Montano is led off.*]
  Iago, look with care about the town
  And silence those whom this vile brawl distracted.   235
  Come, Desdemona: 'tis the soldiers' life
  To have their balmy slumbers waked with strife.
                     [*Exeunt all but Iago and Cassio.*]
Iago: What, are you hurt, lieutenant?
Cassio: Ay, past all surgery.
Iago: Marry, God forbid!   240
Cassio: Reputation, reputation, reputation! O, I have lost my
  reputation! I have lost the immortal part of myself, and what
  remains is bestial. My reputation, Iago, my reputation!
Iago: As I am an honest man, I thought you had received some
  bodily wound. There is more sense in that than in reputation. 245
  Reputation is an idle and most false imposition; oft got
  without merit and lost without deserving. You have lost no
  reputation at all unless you repute yourself such a loser.
  What, man! there are ways to recover the general again.
  You are but now cast in his mood, a punishment more   250
  in policy than in malice, even so as one would beat his
  offenceless dog to affright an imperious lion. Sue to him
  again, and he's yours.
Cassio: I will rather sue to be despised than to deceive so good a
  commander with so slight, so drunken, and so indiscreet an 255
  officer. Drunk? and speak parrot? and squabble? swagger?
  swear? and discourse fustian with one's own shadow? O
  thou invisible spirit of wine, if thou hast no name to be

265   *nothing wherefore:* not the cause of it

267   *pleasance:* enjoyment or pleasure; *applause:* the desire to please

272   *unperfectness:* imperfection

274   *moraler:* moralist or one who moralizes

279   *Hydra:* the nine-headed water snake killed by Hercules as one of his tasks

280   *stop:* close (one's mouth); *by and by:* soon afterwards

281   *inordinate:* immoderate

282   *ingredient:* contents (alcohol or wine)

286   *approved:* proved by experience or test

291   *denotement:* careful observation

292   *importune:* solicit, beg

293   *free:* generous; *apt:* ready, fit

known by, let us call thee devil!

Iago: What was he that you followed with your sword?   260
   What had he done to you?

Cassio: I know not.

Iago: Is't possible?

Cassio: I remember a mass of things, but nothing distinctly; a
   quarrel, but nothing wherefore. O God, that men should   265
   put an enemy in their mouths to steal away their brains!
   that we should with joy, pleasance, revel, and applause
   transform ourselves into beasts!

Iago: Why, but you are now well enough. How came you thus
   recovered?   270

Cassio: It hath pleased the devil drunkenness to give place to the
   devil wrath. One unperfectness shows me another, to make
   me frankly despise myself.

Iago: Come, you are too severe a moraler. As the time, the place,
   and the condition of this country stands, I could heartily   275
   wish this had not so befallen; but since it is as it is, mend it
   for your own good.

Cassio: I will ask him for my place again: he shall tell me I am a
   drunkard! Had I as many mouths as Hydra, such an answer
   would stop them all. To be now a sensible man, by and by   280
   a fool, and presently a beast! O strange! Every inordinate
   cup is unblest, and the ingredient is a devil.

Iago: Come, come, good wine is a good familiar creature if
   it be well used. Exclaim no more against it. And, good
   lieutenant, I think you think I love you.   285

Cassio: I have well approved it, sir. I drunk!

Iago: You or any man living may be drunk at some time, man. I'll
   tell you what you shall do. Our general's wife is now the
   general. I may say so in this respect, for that he hath devoted
   and given up himself to the contemplation, mark, and   290
   denotement of her parts and graces. Confess yourself freely
   to her; importune her help to put you in your place again.
   She is of so free, so kind, so apt, so blessed a disposition she
   holds it a vice in her goodness not to do more than she is
   requested. This broken joint between you and her husband   295

296	*splinter:* bind together, as with splints for a broken bone. *my fortunes ... lay:* I will bet all my possessions against this wager.
297	*this crack ... stronger:* refers to the common belief that a fractured bone, when properly set and healed, is stronger than it was before the injury
301	*I think ... freely:* without reservation; *betimes:* early
302–303	*I am ... here:* I am in despair of my future if my fortunes are held back now (by this incident).

308	*free:* frank, open, honourable, given freely
309	*Probal:* probable, reasonable, credible
311	*inclining:* inclined to be helpful; *subdue:* persuade
312	*suit:* petition; *framed:* fashioned, created; *fruitful:* generous, productive
313	*free elements:* unrestrained elements such as air
314	*win:* win over; *were't:* even were she to ask him
315	*seals ... sin:* The Christian sacraments are the guarantees (seals) and the outward manifestations (symbols) that people may be redeemed and delivered from sin.
316	*enfetter'd:* enslaved, controlled by
317	*list:* likes
318	*her appetite:* her inclination or his irresistible desire for her
319	*weak function:* enslaved natural instincts that diminish his capacity to act because of his fixation on Desdemona
320	*this parallel course:* It seems to lead him in a helpful direction but instead sends him to his destruction.
321	*Divinity of hell:* an argument as good as one that Satan himself might present
322	*put on:* urge, inspire
323	*suggest:* tempt, prompt; *shows:* appearances
325	*Plies:* solicits, begs
327	*pestilence:* a fatal epidemic disease; here, that which is morally poisonous, damning
328	*repeals:* tries to get Cassio returned or recalled from banishment (figuratively)
330	*undo ... Moor:* ruin Othello's faith or belief in her
331	*pitch:* a foul-smelling, black, sticky substance that can, indeed, trap victims

entreat her to splinter; and my fortunes against any lay
worth naming, this crack of your love shall grow stronger
than it was before.

Cassio: You advise me well.

Iago: I protest, in the sincerity of love and honest kindness.   300

Cassio: I think it freely; and betimes in the morning will I beseech
the virtuous Desdemona to undertake for me. I am desperate
of my fortunes if they check me here.

Iago: You are in the right. Good night, lieutenant; I must to the
watch.   305

Cassio: Good night, honest Iago.   [*Exit.*]

Iago: And what's he then that says I play the villain?
When this advice is free I give and honest,
Probal to thinking, and indeed the course
To win the Moor again? For 'tis most easy   310
The inclining Desdemona to subdue
In any honest suit; she's framed as fruitful
As the free elements. And then for her
To win the Moor, were't to renounce his baptism,
All seals and symbols of redeemed sin,   315
His soul is so enfetter'd to her love
That she may make, unmake, do what she list,
Even as her appetite shall play the god
With his weak function. How am I then a villain
To counsel Cassio to this parallel course,   320
Directly to his good? Divinity of hell!
When devils will the blackest sins put on,
They do suggest at first with heavenly shows,
As I do now. For whiles this honest fool
Plies Desdemona to repair his fortunes,   325
And she for him pleads strongly to the Moor,
I'll pour this pestilence into his ear,
That she repeals him for her body's lust;
And by how much she strives to do him good,
She shall undo her credit with the Moor.   330
So will I turn her virtue into pitch,
And out of her own goodness make the net

334	*chase:* the hunt
334–335	*not like ... cry:* In the hunt, there are hounds who "run the scent" (hunt) and those who just follow along making noise. The implication is that Roderigo is one of the "follower" hounds, not actively pursuing. *cry:* pack
336	*cudgelled:* beaten
337	*the issue:* outcome; *so much:* a great deal of
339	*wit:* common sense
342–343	*by wit ... time:* by intelligence and not by magic, for intelligence depends on allowing time to take its necessary course
345	*cashier'd:* dismissed
346–347	*Though ... ripe:* Though other plants grow vigorously in the sunshine, fruit trees that flower first will yield ripe fruit first. That is, though others "grow" in Desdemona's favour, we shall nevertheless succeed in bringing our plot to bear fruit.
353	*move ... mistress:* plead to Desdemona on behalf of Cassio
356	*jump:* at the right moment, exactly at the moment when
358	*Dull ... delay:* Do not let the plan lose its momentum, or do not spoil a great plan by hesitating (delaying) because of lack of enthusiasm.

That shall enmesh them all.

[*Enter Roderigo.*]

How, now, Roderigo?

Roderigo: I do follow here in the chase, not like a hound that
    hunts, but one that fills up the cry. My money is almost   335
    spent; I have been to-night exceedingly well cudgelled; and
    I think the issue will be I shall have so much experience
    for my pains; and so, with no money at all, and a little
    more wit, return again to Venice.

Iago: How poor are they that have not patience!   340
    What wound did ever heal but by degrees?
    Thou know'st we work by wit, and not by witchcraft;
    And wit depends on dilatory time.
    Does't not go well? Cassio hath beaten thee,
    And thou by that small hurt hast cashier'd Cassio.   345
    Though other things grow fair against the sun,
    Yet fruits that blossom first will first be ripe.
    Content thyself awhile. By the mass, 'tis morning!
    Pleasure and action make the hours seem short.
    Retire thee; go where thou art billeted.   350
    Away, I say! Thou shalt know more hereafter.
    Nay, get thee gone!   [*Exit Roderigo.*]

Two things are to be done:
    My wife must move for Cassio to her mistress;
    I'll set her on;
    Myself the while to draw the Moor apart   355
    And bring him jump when he may Cassio find
    Soliciting his wife. Ay, that's the way!
    Dull not device by coldness and delay.   [*Exit.*]

Act 2, Scene 3: Activities

1. This is an extremely long scene. If you were to cut the scene in half, what would you cut, and why?

2. This time, Iago executes the biggest trick in his book so far. What is it? How can he get away with it? If Cassio is supposedly an astute second-in-command to Othello, why would he succumb to a known vulnerability? Is Roderigo's behaviour predictable in this situation? Create and present a TV script based on this segment of the scene. Remember, what is said in the script is not always what comes across to an audience.

3. Montano is the man Othello is to replace as military leader in Cyprus. What does his conversation with Iago tell you about his ability to "read" people? In your opinion, would Montano have made a good governor had Othello not appeared? Can you possibly admire Iago's machinations here? How important is it to be able to read people? Discuss this with your group, and then record your views in a journal entry. You might want to sketch a plot for a short story on this subject.

4. In his soliloquy at the end of the scene, Iago reveals more about how his mind works. What are his plans this time? If you were filming his speech as part of a movie you were directing, how would you present it without making the whole thing appear artificial? Why would you include this speech anyway—does it have anything at all to do with advancing the play?

5. Cassio is either terribly naïve or incredibly ambitious. Or he may be neither of these. What is your assessment of him? If he contacted you by e-mail asking for advice, what would you tell him? How would you word your response?

6. The staged (and planned) fight scene between Cassio and Roderigo seems to have worked for Iago and appears to further his plans. Iago, of course, says nothing at all to implicate himself. Write a diary or journal entry that Iago might have written about his success in causing Cassio's downfall.

7. In this scene Othello seems to lose his usual calm. Why does that happen? After all, it was his party and he had it announced to the general populace. Why do you think a military man of

Othello's experience would be so incensed about what we might dismiss as just a disagreement among people at a party? If you haven't kept a profile of Othello, perhaps this is a good time to begin. Develop your character portrait of Othello and figure out, in your journal, what makes him "tick."

8. Hate is generally considered to be a terrible and destructive motivator. In your group, discuss why Iago is so driven by this passion. You could write a magazine article or an editorial in which you air your thoughts on this topic. Perhaps not everyone would believe that Iago is entirely unjustified in his behaviour. How would you defend that position?

9. Iago gives a speech (line 319) in which he says, "How am I then a villain...?" What is your notion of a villain? How would you describe one? Is Iago really what he says he is? With your group, talk about some of the great "villains" you know about from films or from history. Write an account, based on research, of villains in history and decide in your conclusion whether villains are essentially born "villainous" or if they become that way. Have you ever encountered a true villain? Is there really such a thing as a villain, or is it just a state of mind? Develop a script for a documentary on the subject of villains, and present it to the class.

10. Write a letter to Cassio, Roderigo, or Othello warning about Iago's intentions to use them for his own purposes. How would you convince the subject of your letter that you actually know what you are talking about?

11. Thanks to the miracle of time-travel, you and your partner have landed in the midst of this scene. Recreate the dialogue that the two of you engaged in as you watched this episode unfold.

12. With a partner, role-play the episode between Roderigo and Iago in which Roderigo complains bitterly that nothing is turning out well for him. Decide, in your journal, how anybody could possibly be as oblivious to what is really going on as Roderigo.

13. Create a photo essay that captures all of the significant events covered in this scene. You can use cut-outs from old magazines, cartoons from newspapers, drawings of your own, or photographs to make your story come alive.

14. With a partner, cluster what you consider to be the key images from this scene. Using quotations where you can, create a narrative poem that succinctly tells the story. You might try a rap or invent some other unconventional form to make it all work. Perform your final result to your group or the class.

15. At one point, Iago says, "By the mass, 'tis morning; Pleasure and action make the hours seem short" (line 348). How do you interpret his comment? Under what circumstances could you have made such a comment? In your journal, record, as Iago, exactly what you meant and what you had been doing to cause you to make such a remark.

16. Cassio goes on about the evils of drinking in this scene (for example, line 265). What does he say? Use a picture of Cassio and part of his speech in a poster condemning alcohol abuse. Does Cassio see this as a social problem or a personal one? Why does he use the images he does? If he knows his own limitations with alcohol, why does he succumb to Iago's entreaties? Where did the images he uses come from? Since he has just been named Othello's lieutenant, why would he even contemplate jeopardizing his position by committing an indiscretion of such magnitude? Is he gullible or just weak?

17. What really causes the fight between Roderigo and Cassio? Does either of them have a cause for attacking the other? In an interview with both of them afterward, present their arguments for such an engagement despite dire warnings from Othello. Is Othello in any way responsible for what happened?

18. As a journalist, how would you cover the fight between Roderigo and Cassio in a brief but telling account for the six o'clock news broadcast? Script what you would say carefully so that you do not appear to be biased. Try your scripted version in your group before you present it to the class.

Act 2: Consider the Whole Act

1. Most of the characters seem to be caught up in themselves to the exclusion of just about everything else in Act 2. What are

some of the things that seem to consume them? Write a newspaper advice column pointing out the dangers of this kind of short-sighted, self-indulgent point of view.

2. Write an instructional pamphlet titled "How To Read Shakespeare" using this act to illustrate your approach. What pointers can you offer readers who are new to Shakespeare?

3. Choose *one* speech by any character in this act, and change it so it might alter the entire outcome of Iago's seemingly successful plans. Alternatively, you could write a new speech that would change the course of the action.

4. In order to visualize what has happened, create a sketch, collage, or storyboard to capture the progress of the whole act.

5. You are the host of a talk show and your guest has played Cassio in a new film version of *Othello*. You are going to show a clip of it to your audience. What speech or action from Act 2 featuring Cassio do you choose to present? Explain your choice.

6. Read the story of Pandora, the woman in Greek mythology who brought misery to humanity by opening a forbidden box that had been given to her by Zeus. Iago seems to possess his own version of Pandora's box, and like Pandora he seems intent on opening it—when he feels the time is right. As Iago, decide what might be the "right" time to do this. Why would you want to do such a thing? What do you, as Iago, gain from such an act? Write a new version of the Pandora myth, substituting Iago for Pandora. Would Iago and Pandora have made a suitable couple?

For the next scene ...

Sometimes people attempt to gain someone's affections or favour by asking another person to mediate for them. Many situation comedies use this technique. Describe one of these occurrences either from TV or from your personal experience. What was the outcome?

Act 3, Scene 1

In this scene ...

Cassio appears the next morning with some musicians outside the castle to honour Othello and Desdemona. A messenger from Othello arrives to have the music stopped, and Cassio uses the opportunity to ask the messenger to deliver a message to Emilia asking her to speak with him about obtaining Desdemona's assistance. Iago enters and promises to enlist Emilia's aid on Cassio's behalf and to keep Othello out of the way during their conversation. Emilia enters and assures Cassio that Othello still holds him in high regard and that Desdemona is already pleading with Othello to reinstate him. Cassio nonetheless proceeds with his plan to plead his case directly to Desdemona alone.

1	*content your pains:* reward you for your trouble
2	*Good morrow:* the standard greeting to meet (or wake) the bride and groom after the wedding night; Stage Direction: *Clown*—a peasant or fool or jester (as part of the household, perhaps) or just a servant with a budding sense of humour
3–4	*have ... nose thus:* Possibly, this is a reference to Naples and its reputation as a place where one could contract syphilis and other sexual diseases. Syphilis could eat away the bridge of the nose.
6–10	The clown is making a tasteless joke with the terms "wind" and "tail."

23	*Prithee ... quillets:* Put aside your arguments, disagreements, or petty objections. "Quillets" means quibbles.

Act 3, Scene 1

Before the castle.
Enter Cassio and some Musicians.

Cassio: Masters, play here, I will content your pains:
    Something that's brief; and bid "Good morrow, general."
                                      [Music.]

[Enter the Clown.]

Clown: Why, masters, have your instruments been in Naples,
    that they speak i' the nose thus?
First Musician: How, sir, how?   5
Clown: Are these, I pray you, wind instruments?
First Musician: Ay, marry, are they, sir.
Clown: O, thereby hangs a tail.
First Musician: Whereby hangs a tale, sir?
Clown: Marry, sir, by many a wind instrument that I know. But,   10
    masters, here's money for you; and the general so likes your
    music that he desires you, for love's sake, to make no more
    noise with it.
First Musician: Well, sir, we will not.
Clown: If you have any music that may not be heard, to't again: 15
    but, as they say, to hear music the general does not greatly
    care.
First Musician: We have none such, sir.
Clown: Then put up your pipes in your bag, for I'll away. Go,
    vanish into air, away!   *[Exeunt Musicians.]*   20
Cassio: Dost thou hear, my honest friend?
Clown: No, I hear not your honest friend. I hear you.
Cassio: Prithee keep up thy quillets. There's a poor piece of gold for
    thee. If the gentlewoman that attends the general's wife be

25–26	*a little ... speech:* the honour of speaking with her
27–28	*shall seem to notify:* shall have notified her
29	*In happy time:* at the appropriate moment
33	*send in:* deliver a message; *suit:* petition
35	*access:* an audience with; *presently:* immediately
36	*a mean:* a means
40	*A Florentine:* Possibly, Cassio, a Florentine, praises Iago as a kind and honest man—as honest and decent as one of Cassio's own townspeople.
42	*displeasure:* difficulty, unhappiness, loss of favour
45	*he you hurt:* meaning Montano
46	*affinity:* powerful family or familial connections
47	*might not but refuse:* could only refuse, dismiss, or refuse to appoint
48	*suitor:* the person bringing the suit or petition
49	*front:* literally, "forelock," referring to hair falling over the face; possibly, "grab the earliest opportunity"
50	*bring you in again:* give you back your former position
51	*or that:* and if

stirring, tell her there's one Cassio entreats her a little favour 25
    of speech. Wilt thou do this?

Clown: She is stirring, sir. If she will stir hither, I shall seem to
    notify unto her.

Cassio: Do, good my friend.   *[Exit Clown.]*

  [Enter Iago.]

                  In happy time, Iago.

Iago: You have not been a-bed then?   30

Cassio: Why, no; the day had broke
  Before we parted. I have made bold, Iago,
  To send in to your wife: my suit to her
  Is that she will to virtuous Desdemona
  Procure me some access.

Iago: I'll send her to you presently;   35
  And I'll devise a mean to draw the Moor
  Out of the way, that your converse and business
  May be more free.

Cassio: I humbly thank you for't   *[Exit Iago.]*
                 I never knew
  A Florentine more kind and honest.   40

  [Enter Emilia.]

Emilia: Good morrow, good lieutenant. I am sorry
  For your displeasure; but all will sure be well.
  The general and his wife are talking of it,
  And she speaks for you stoutly. The Moor replies
  That he you hurt is of great fame in Cyprus   45
  And great affinity, and that in wholesome wisdom
  He might not but refuse you; but he protests he loves you,
  And needs no other suitor but his likings
  To take the safest occasion by the front
  To bring you in again.

Cassio: Yet I beseech you,   50
  If you think fit, or that it may be done,
  Give me advantage of some brief discourse
  With Desdemona alone.

54   *bestow:* put you in a place; *time:* opportunity
55   *bosom:* your innermost thoughts

Emilia: Pray you come in.
 I will bestow you where you shall have time
 To speak your bosom freely.
Cassio: I am much bound to you. 55
          [*Exeunt.*]

Act 3, Scene 1: Activities

1. This scene is cut by some directors, but is included by others. What decision would you make? Consider the following:

   - Does it provide a transition from Act 2, Scene 3?
   - Is the content significant enough that it demands attention as a scene on its own?
   - Does it connect at all with Act 3, Scene 2?
   - Does its content warrant audience attention?

   First, decide what the scene is all about, looking up references that are not clear. If, as some directors claim, the scene is needed for "comic relief," why is comic relief necessary at this point? If you do not agree that it is necessary, how would you, as director, handle the transition between Act 2, Scene 3 and Act 3, Scene 2? If it isn't about comic relief, then what is it about?

   Before you make a decision, you should discuss this with your group and perhaps engage in a discussion with other groups about how to deal with this issue. You could then, collectively, share your conclusions with the entire class.

2. Decide in your group why Cassio confides in Iago about his plan to have Desdemona intercede with Othello on his behalf. If you could project yourself into this scene and take Cassio aside, what would you say to him?

3. Write a soliloquy for Iago after his conversation with Cassio, keeping in mind that Iago has revealed nothing of himself to anybody in the play so far.

For the next scene ...

What makes an excellent employee? Describe what you think are the most important qualities a person should have in order to function successfully in a job. Apply your criteria to Othello in the next scene.

Act 3, Scene 2

In this scene ...

This short scene shows Iago taking a message from Othello to the pilot of the ship that is returning to Venice and then arranging to meet the general later on the castle ramparts.

1	*pilot:* presumably the pilot of the ship that brought Othello to Cyprus
2	*by him:* through him, by means of his assistance; *do my duties:* pay my respects
3	*works:* defensive fortifications, ramparts
4	*Repair:* come, make your way
6	*wait upon:* attend

Scene 2

A room in the castle.
Enter Othello, Iago, and Gentlemen.

Othello: These letters give, Iago, to the pilot,
   And by him do my duties to the Senate.
   That done, I will be walking on the works;
   Repair there to me.
Iago: Well, my good lord, I'll do't.
Othello: This fortification, gentlemen, shall we see't?   5
Gentlemen: We'll wait upon your lordship.   [*Exeunt.*]

Act 3, Scene 2: Activities

1. This scene has only six lines. What does it establish that warrants it being an entire scene on its own? In a short essay, decide what possible need there is to even include this scene. You might want to look at the setting and consider Othello's position in Cyprus. You might also consider this scene's connection to the previous scene, if there is one. Does it connect to the scene that follows? How would you stage such a brief scene?

For the next scene ...

How can people plant seeds of suspicion in the minds
of others? Why would anyone want to do such a thing?
Do you think people basically trust each other? Can this
be a problem?

Act 3, Scene 3

In this scene ...

Desdemona, Emilia, and Cassio meet in the castle garden, but the meeting is cut short by the arrival of Othello and Iago. Cassio, ashamed of his earlier behaviour, hurries away to avoid speaking with Othello, and Iago suggests that Cassio's hasty exit is suspicious. Desdemona begs Othello to call Cassio back and give him some hope of reinstatement. Othello refuses, but when Desdemona persists, he does agree to see Cassio. When Iago is alone with Othello, he plays on his imagination, creating in him an uneasiness about Desdemona's faithfulness, and he warns Othello against succumbing to jealousy. Othello wants proof, and Iago advises him to watch Desdemona with Cassio. Othello protests Desdemona's innocence, and Iago warns that he should not be too hasty to restore Cassio to favour so he can observe to what lengths Desdemona will go on Cassio's behalf. When Desdemona enters and Othello complains of a headache, she offers to soothe it by wrapping her handkerchief around his head. Othello refuses the handkerchief as being too small, and it falls to the ground. Emilia picks it up and plans to give a copy of it to Iago. Just at that moment, Iago enters and takes it from her. We learn that he plans to plant it in Cassio's house. Othello re-enters, now consumed by jealousy, and he threatens Iago with death if he does not immediately offer proof of Desdemona's unfaithfulness. Iago claims that he overheard Cassio talking in his sleep one night about making love to Desdemona, and he also says that he has seen Cassio wipe his beard with her handkerchief. Othello is now enraged and vows to kill his wife for her infidelity. He orders Cassio killed within three days. He then says to Iago, "Now art thou my lieutenant."

2	*All my abilities:* everything I can
3	*I warrant:* I assure you

12–13	*in strangeness ... politic distance:* be cold to you only because it is politically wise or expedient to do so
15–16	*Or feed ... of circumstance:* The lines are not clear, but they suggest the reasons why Cassio is afraid to wait for Othello to accept him into his good graces once again.
17	*supplied:* filled
19	*doubt:* fear; *before:* in the presence of
20	*give thee warrant:* give you assurance or a guarantee, as in to make a pledge; *thy place:* your position as lieutenant; *Assure thee:* be assured or certain
21	*a friendship:* an act of friendship
23	*I'll ... tame:* keep him awake at night until he agrees. The reference is to the training of hawks, which were tamed by being kept awake.
24	*his ... shrift:* His table (board) shall seem to be a place of confession (shrift).

Scene 3

The garden of the castle.
Enter Desdemona, Cassio, and Emilia.

Desdemona: Be thou assured, good Cassio, I will do
   All my abilities in thy behalf.
Emilia: Good madam, do. I warrant it grieves my husband
   As if the cause were his.
Desdemona: O, that's an honest fellow. Do not doubt, Cassio,   5
   But I will have my lord and you again
   As friendly as you were.
Cassio: Bounteous madam,
   Whatever shall become of Michael Cassio,
   He's never any thing but your true servant.
Desdemona: I know't; I thank you. You do love my lord;   10
   You have known him long; and be you well assured
   He shall in strangeness stand no farther off
   Than in a politic distance.
Cassio: Ay, but, lady,
   That policy may either last so long,
   Or feed upon such nice and waterish diet,   15
   Or breed itself so out of circumstance,
   That, I being absent, and my place supplied,
   My general will forget my love and service.
Desdemona: Do not doubt that; before Emilia here
   I give thee warrant of thy place. Assure thee,   20
   If I do vow a friendship, I'll perform it
   To the last article. My lord shall never rest;
   I'll watch him tame and talk him out of patience;
   His bed shall seem a school, his board a shrift;
   I'll intermingle everything he does   25
   With Cassio's suit. Therefore be merry, Cassio,

28   *give thy cause away:* lose your case or suit or give up your cause

33   *Unfit for mine own purposes:* unable to plead my own cause
34   *do your discretion:* act according your own discretion, behave as you see fit

42   *suitor:* petitioner, also lover

47   *His ... take:* make effective his immediate return (restoration) to office and your favour
49   *in cunning:* knowingly, deliberately
50   *in:* of

52   *sooth:* a polite or mild oath as in "in truth"

For thy solicitor shall rather die
Than give thy cause away.

[*Enter Othello and Iago, at a distance.*]

Emilia: Madam, here comes my lord.
Cassio: Madam, I'll take my leave.   30
Desdemona: Why, stay, and hear me speak.
Cassio: Madam, not now: I am very ill at ease,
   Unfit for mine own purposes.
Desdemona: Well, do your discretion.   [*Exit Cassio.*]
Iago: Ha! I like not that.
Othello: What dost thou say?   35
Iago: Nothing, my lord; or if—I know not what.
Othello: Was not that Cassio parted from my wife?
Iago: Cassio, my lord? No, sure, I cannot think it,
   That he would steal away so guilty-like,
   Seeing you coming.
Othello: I do believe 'twas he.   40
Desdemona: How now, my lord?
   I have been talking with a suitor here,
   A man that languishes in your displeasure.
Othello: Who is't you mean?
Desdemona: Why, your lieutenant, Cassio. Good my lord,   45
   If I have any grace or power to move you,
   His present reconciliation take;
   For if he be not one that truly loves you,
   That errs in ignorance, and not in cunning,
   I have no judgement in an honest face.   50
   I prithee call him back.
Othello: Went he hence now?
Desdemona: Ay, sooth; so humbled
   That he hath left part of his grief with me
   To suffer with him. Good love, call him back.
Othello: Not now, sweet Desdemon; some other time.   55
Desdemona: But shall't be shortly?
Othello: The sooner, sweet, for you.
Desdemona: Shall't be to-night at supper?

58   *dinner:* then, the midday meal

64   *in our common reason:* according to the general way of
            thinking, or what common sense dictates
65–66   *the wars ... their best:* the military profession must punish
            even their best men as examples
66   *not almost:* barely, hardly, scarcely
67   *a private check:* a personal censure or rebuke (which
            Cassio is enduring along with his public disgrace)
70   *mammering:* hesitating, stuttering, muttering

72   *dispraisingly:* in unflattering terms

76   *boon:* great favour

79   *a peculiar profit:* something of special advantage or personal
            good for yourself
80   *To your own person:* the same idea as line 79, repeated for
            emphasis and insistence
81   *to touch:* test
82   *poise:* importance or significance
83   *fearful to be granted:* with fear it might not be granted
84   *Whereon:* in return for what I have just told you

87   *straight:* immediately or at once
88   *fancies:* wishes or desires

Othello: No, not to-night.

Desdemona: To-morrow dinner then?

Othello: I shall not dine at home;
   I meet the captains at the citadel.

Desdemona: Why then, to-morrow night, or Tuesday morn,   60
   On Tuesday noon or night, on Wednesday morn.
   I prithee name the time, but let it not
   Exceed three days. In faith, he's penitent;
   And yet his trespass, in our common reason—
   Save that, they say, the wars must make examples   65
   Out of their best—is not almost a fault
   To incur a private check. When shall he come?
   Tell me, Othello. I wonder in my soul
   What you could ask me that I should deny
   Or stand so mammering on. What? Michael Cassio,   70
   That came a-wooing with you, and so many a time,
   When I have spoke of you dispraisingly,
   Hath ta'en your part—to have so much to do
   To bring him in? Trust me, I could do much—

Othello: Prithee, no more. Let him come when he will.   75
   I will deny thee nothing.

Desdemona: Why, this is not a boon;
   'Tis as I should entreat you wear your gloves,
   Or feed on nourishing dishes, or keep you warm,
   Or sue to you to do a peculiar profit
   To your own person. Nay, when I have a suit   80
   Wherein I mean to touch your love indeed,
   It shall be full of poise and difficult weight,
   And fearful to be granted.

Othello: I will deny thee nothing.
   Whereon I do beseech thee grant me this,
   To leave me but a little to myself.   85

Desdemona: Shall I deny you? No. Farewell, my lord.

Othello: Farewell, my Desdemon: I'll come to thee straight.

Desdemona: Emilia, come. Be as your fancies teach you;
   Whate'er you be, I am obedient.

                        [*Exeunt Desdemona and Emilia.*]

91	*But:* unless
91–92	*when ... come again:* I will love you until the time the universe once again is overcome or consumed by chaos (confusion).

111	*of my counsel:* in my confidence

115	*conceit:* idea, thought

118	*for:* because

Othello: Excellent wretch! Perdition catch my soul 90
  But I do love thee! and when I love thee not,
  Chaos is come again.
Iago: My noble lord—
Othello: What dost thou say, Iago?
Iago: Did Michael Cassio, when you woo'd my lady,
  Know of your love? 95
Othello: He did, from first to last. Why dost thou ask?
Iago: But for a satisfaction of my thought;
  No further harm.
Othello: Why of thy thought, Iago?
Iago: I did not think he had been acquainted with her.
Othello: O, yes, and went between us very oft. 100
Iago: Indeed?
Othello: Indeed? Ay, indeed! Discern'st thou aught in that?
  Is he not honest?
Iago: Honest, my lord?
Othello: Honest. Ay, honest.
Iago: My lord, for aught I know.
Othello: What dost thou think?
Iago: Think, my lord?
Othello: Think, my lord? 105
  By heaven, he echoes me,
  As if there were some monster in his thought
  Too hideous to be shown. Thou dost mean something;
  I heard thee say even now, thou likedst not that,
  When Cassio left my wife. What didst not like? 110
  And when I told thee he was of my counsel
  In my whole course of wooing, thou criedst "Indeed?"
  And didst contract and purse thy brow together,
  As if thou then hadst shut up in thy brain
  Some horrible conceit. If thou dost love me, 115
  Show me thy thought.
Iago: My lord, you know I love you.
Othello: I think thou dost;
  And, for I know thou'rt full of love and honesty
  And weigh'st thy words before thou givest them breath

120   *stops:* pauses, hesitations

122   *tricks of custom:* usual tricks, or tricks usually employed

123   *close dilations:* expressions of secret feelings welling up from inside, or expressions of hidden thoughts

124   *That ... rule:* that are not governed by the emotions; *For:* as for

127   *seem none:* not pretend (to be honest)

128   *Certain:* certainly

135   *that ... free to:* tell what even slaves may keep to themselves or are free with respect to

137   *whereinto:* into which

139   *uncleanly apprehensions:* impure thoughts

140   *Keep ... days:* hold court; referring to meetings of local courts; *law-days:* days when court was in session

140–141 *in session sit with:* sit together with

145   *vicious:* defective, mistaken

147   *jealousy:* suspicion

148   *Shapes:* imagines

148–150 *that your ... no notice:* that you, in your wisdom, would take no notice of

151   *observance:* observation

152   *It were not for:* it is not in the interest of or would not be conducive to

Therefore these stops of thine fright me the more;   120
For such things in a false disloyal knave
Are tricks of custom; but in a man that's just
They are close dilations, working from the heart
That passion cannot rule.

Iago: For Michael Cassio,
  I dare be sworn I think that he is honest.   125

Othello: I think so too.

Iago: Men should be what they seem;
  Or those that be not, would they might seem none!

Othello: Certain, men should be what they seem.

Iago: Why then, I think Cassio's an honest man.

Othello: Nay, yet there's more in this.   130
  I prithee, speak to me as to thy thinkings,
  As thou dost ruminate, and give thy worst of thoughts
  The worst of words.

Iago: Good my lord, pardon me:
  Though I am bound to every act of duty,
  I am not bound to that all slaves are free to.   135
  Utter my thoughts? Why, say they are vile and false,
  As where's that palace whereinto foul things
  Sometimes intrude not? Who has a breast so pure
  But some uncleanly apprehensions
  Keep leets and law-days, and in session sit   140
  With meditations lawful?

Othello: Thou dost conspire against thy friend, Iago,
  If thou but think'st him wrong'd, and makest his ear
  A stranger to thy thoughts.

Iago: I do beseech you—
  Though I perchance am vicious in my guess,   145
  As, I confess, it is my nature's plague
  To spy into abuses, and oft my jealousy
  Shapes faults that are not—that your wisdom yet
  From one that so imperfectly conceits,
  Would take no notice, nor build yourself a trouble   150
  Out of his scattering and unsure observance.
  It were not for your quiet nor your good,

155–156   *Good ... their souls:* A good name is the most precious part of the soul.

166–167   *doth mock ... feeds on:* plays with its victim or teases, as a cat does a mouse

168   *Who, certain of his fate:* who, though certain that his wife is unfaithful; *his wronger:* the person doing the wrong (his wife or, perhaps, her lover)

169   *tells he o'er:* does he count

172   *Poor:* the person who is poor

173   *fineless:* without limit

174   *ever:* always

178   *still:* constantly or continually

180   *once to be resolved:* to find out the truth immediately (at once)

186   *Where virtue is ... virtuous:* When a woman is virtuous, these are virtuous achievements.

Nor for my manhood, honesty, or wisdom,
To let you know my thoughts.
Othello: What dost thou mean?
Iago: Good name in man and woman, dear my lord,   155
  Is the immediate jewel of their souls.
  Who steals my purse steals trash; 'tis something, nothing;
  'Twas mine, 'tis his, and has been slave to thousands;
  But he that filches from me my good name
  Robs me of that which not enriches him   160
  And makes me poor indeed.
Othello: By heaven, I'll know thy thoughts!
Iago: You cannot, if my heart were in your hand;
  Nor shall not whilst 'tis in my custody.
Othello: Ha!
Iago: O, beware, my lord, of jealousy;   165
  It is the green-eyed monster, which doth mock
  The meat it feeds on. That cuckold lives in bliss
  Who, certain of his fate, loves not his wronger;
  But oh, what damned minutes tells he o'er
  Who dotes, yet doubts, suspects, yet strongly loves!   170
Othello: O misery!
Iago: Poor and content is rich, and rich enough;
  But riches fineless is as poor as winter
  To him that ever fears he shall be poor.
  Good heaven, the souls of all my tribe defend   175
  From jealousy!
Othello: Why, why is this?
  Think'st thou I'ld make a life of jealousy,
  To follow still the changes of the moon
  With fresh suspicions? No; to be once in doubt
  Is once to be resolved. Exchange me for a goat   180
  When I shall turn the business of my soul
  To such exsufflicate and blown surmises,
  Matching thy inference. 'Tis not to make me jealous
  To say my wife is fair, feeds well, loves company,
  Is free of speech, sings, plays, and dances well;   185
  Where virtue is, these are more virtuous;

188	*doubt of her revolt:* suspicion of her unfaithfulness

| 190 | *prove:* put it to the test and prove it one way or the other |
| 191 | *on the proof:* when I have proof |

198	*not jealous nor secure:* neither totally suspicious nor totally trustful
200	*self-bounty:* inherent kindness and generosity; *abused:* tricked or deceived; *Look to't:* watch out, be on guard
201–204	*our country ... unknown:* Venetian women were reputed to be skilled at deception and having affairs.

208	*go to:* an expression of annoyance, like "come on!"
209	*give out such a seeming:* put on such a fake appearance
210	*seel:* close up, a falconry term meaning to cover the eyes in the process of taming. *close as oak:* Oak is a very hard, dense, close-grained wood that is difficult to penetrate.
212	*of:* for

217	*moved:* troubled
218	*am to:* must
218–220	*strain my speech ... suspicion:* expand on what I say so that it has more implications or consequences than to raise suspicion

Nor from mine own weak merits will I draw
The smallest fear or doubt of her revolt,
For she had eyes, and chose me. No, Iago;
I'll see before I doubt; when I doubt, prove;   190
And on the proof there is no more but this—
Away at once with love or jealousy!
Iago: I am glad of this; for now I shall have reason
To show the love and duty that I bear you
With franker spirit. Therefore, as I am bound   195
Receive it from me. I speak not yet of proof.
Look to your wife; observe her well with Cassio;
Wear your eye thus, not jealous nor secure:
I would not have your free and noble nature,
Out of self-bounty, be abused. Look to't.   200
I know our country disposition well:
In Venice they do let heaven see the pranks
They dare not show their husbands; their best conscience
Is not to leave't undone, but keep't unknown.
Othello: Dost thou say so?   205
Iago: She did deceive her father, marrying you;
And when she seem'd to shake and fear your looks,
She loved them most.
Othello: And so she did.
Iago: Why, go to then;
She that, so young, could give out such a seeming
To seel her father's eyes up close as oak—   210
He thought 'twas witchcraft—but I am much to blame.
I humbly do beseech you of your pardon
For too much loving you.
Othello: I am bound to thee for ever.
Iago: I see this hath a little dash'd your spirits.
Othello: Not a jot, not a jot.
Iago: I' faith, I fear it has.   215
I hope you will consider what is spoke
Comes from my love. But I do see you're moved.
I am to pray you not to strain my speech
To grosser issues nor to larger reach

222	*fall ... success:* have such an undesirable, nasty outcome
225	*I do not think but:* I do not think that Desdemona is anything other than (but) honest, chaste, or honourable.
227	*erring from itself:* behaving unnaturally; wandering from her God-given nature (sinning)
229	*affect:* prefer, be attracted to, or encourage
230	*clime:* region or country, suggesting those things that determine the nature of a person, including skin colour and rank; *complexion:* skin colour and temperament; *degree:* social rank (a play on the word "rank" (smelly); implying lust)
231	*Whereto:* to which
232	*such:* such a person; *will:* desire, in the carnal sense; *rank:* excessive, lustful, as in "in heat"
234–235	*in position ... of her:* making this proposal or proposition speak specifically of her
236	*recoiling:* returning, or giving way to
237	*fall to match:* happen to compare; *country forms:* the forms (appearances) of those from her own country
238	*happily:* perhaps
240	*Set on:* urge
243	*unfolds:* reveals
244	*would I might:* I would like to
246	*place:* position as lieutenant
249	*his means:* his methods (to recover his lost position)
250	*strain his entertainment:* insist on his reinstatement
253	*busy:* meddlesome, officious, or inquisitive

Than to suspicion. 220
Othello: I will not.
Iago: Should you do so, my lord,
  My speech should fall into such vile success
  As my thoughts aim not at. Cassio's my worthy friend—
  My lord, I see you're moved.
Othello: No, not much moved:
  I do not think but Desdemona's honest. 225
Iago: Long live she so! and long live you to think so!
Othello: And yet, how nature erring from itself—
Iago: Ay, there's the point. As to be bold with you—
  Not to affect many proposed matches
  Of her own clime, complexion, and degree, 230
  Whereto we see in all things nature tends—
  Foh! one may smell in such a will most rank,
  Foul disproportion, thoughts unnatural.
  But pardon me. I do not in position
  Distinctly speak of her; though I may fear 235
  Her will, recoiling to her better judgement,
  May fall to match you with her country forms,
  And happily repent.
Othello: Farewell, farewell!
  If more thou dost perceive, let me know more.
  Set on thy wife to observe. Leave me, Iago. 240
Iago: My lord, I take my leave.   *[Going.]*
Othello: Why did I marry? This honest creature doubtless
  Sees and knows more, much more, than he unfolds.
Iago: [*Returning.*] My lord, I would I might entreat your honour
  To scan this thing no further; leave it to time. 245
  Although 'tis fit that Cassio have his place,
  For sure he fills it up with great ability,
  Yet, if you please to hold him off awhile,
  You shall by that perceive him and his means.
  Note if your lady strain his entertainment 250
  With any strong or vehement importunity;
  Much will be seen in that. In the mean time
  Let me be thought too busy in my fears—

254   *As worthy ... I am:* I have great or good reason to fear that I am. "Worthy" means good.

255   *hold her free:* consider her innocent or guiltless

256   *Fear not my government:* do not feel uneasy about the way I will handle or manage this. "Government" means manage, as in "govern."

259   *qualities:* kinds, characters, or natures; *with a learned spirit:* with a mind well informed or experienced

260   *Of human dealings:* "Dealings" has implications of intercourse, so the two lines suggest something like "He has a mind experienced in all kinds of human behaviour," including the depraved. *haggard:* wild, uncontrolled, unchaste. A haggard is a wild female falcon captured as an adult.

261   *Though that:* even if; *jesses:* straps tied around the legs of a hawk and attached to the wrist of the falconer for control

262   *whistle ... the wind:* Falcons were set in flight by a whistle and against the wind when they were pursuing prey. A falcon let loose was "whistled down the wind," meaning it was allowed to go with the wind. In this context it suggests that Desdemona is too wild to tame. To "go down the wind" also meant that someone was difficult or out of control.

263   *prey at fortune:* fend for herself as fortune wills; *Haply, for:* perhaps because

264   *soft parts:* social graces

265   *chamberers:* These were "gallants" or social "gentlemen" who pursued ladies of quality for all sorts of reasons and purposes.

266   *vale of years:* probably an allusion to the biblical valley of the shadow of death or "vale of tears"

267   *abused:* tricked, deceived, or wronged

273   *great ones:* people of high social position

274   *Prerogatived ... the base:* Men of the highest ranks are not exempt from having wives who are unfaithful any more than those of lower ranks.

276   *this forked plague:* a reference to wearing the horns (goat horns) designating a cuckold, husband who has an unfaithful wife

277   *do quicken:* are conceived or born

280   *generous:* noble or high-born

282   *to blame:* at fault

284   *upon my forehead:* a gesture, presumably, to indicate where the horns of the cuckold protrude

285   *with watching:* from lack of sleep

As worthy cause I have to fear I am—
And hold her free, I do beseech your honour.   255
Othello: Fear not my government.
Iago: I once more take my leave.   [*Exit.*]
Othello: This fellow's of exceeding honesty,
    And knows all qualities, with a learned spirit
    Of human dealings. If I do prove her haggard,   260
    Though that her jesses were my dear heartstrings,
    I'ld whistle her off and let her down the wind
    To prey at fortune. Haply, for I am black
    And have not those soft parts of conversation
    That chamberers have, or for I am declined   265
    Into the vale of years—yet that's not much—
    She's gone. I am abused, and my relief
    Must be to loathe her. O curse of marriage,
    That we can call these delicate creatures ours,
    And not their appetites! I had rather be a toad   270
    And live upon the vapour of a dungeon
    Than keep a corner in the thing I love
    For others' uses. Yet 'tis the plague of great ones;
    Prerogatived are they less than the base.
    'Tis destiny unshunnable, like death.   275
    Even then this forked plague is fated to us
    When we do quicken. Look where she comes.

[*Enter Desdemona and Emilia.*]

    If she be false, O, then heaven mocks itself!
    I'll not believe't.
Desdemona: How now, my dear Othello?
    Your dinner, and the generous islanders   280
    By you invited, do attend your presence.
Othello: I am to blame.
Desdemona: Why do you speak so faintly?
    Are you not well?
Othello: I have a pain upon my forehead, here.
Desdemona: Faith, that's with watching; 'twill away again.   285
    Let me but bind it hard, within this hour

287 *napkin:* handkerchief

288 *it:* his forehead or headache

291 *remembrance:* keepsake, gift of sentimental value

294 *conjured:* requested humbly; *ever:* always
295 *reserves it evermore:* keeps it forever
296 *work ta'en out:* the pattern copied, probably a reference to
    needlework, embroidery

299 *nothing but:* only wish; *fantasy:* whim

312 *to the advantage:* taking advantage of the opportunity

316 *purpose of import:* important purpose

It will be well.

Othello: Your napkin is too little;
        [*He puts the handkerchief from him, and she drops it.*]
  Let it alone. Come, I'll go in with you.

Desdemona: I am very sorry that you are not well.
                [*Exeunt Othello and Desdemona.*]

Emilia: I am glad I have found this napkin;   290
  This was her first remembrance from the Moor.
  My wayward husband hath a hundred times
  Woo'd me to steal it; but she so loves the token,
  For he conjured her she should ever keep it,
  That she reserves it evermore about her   295
  To kiss and talk to. I'll have the work ta'en out
  And give't Iago: what he will do with it
  Heaven knows, not I;
  I nothing but to please his fantasy.

  [*Re-enter Iago.*]

Iago: How now? What do you here alone?   300
Emilia: Do not you chide; I have a thing for you.
Iago: A thing for me? It is a common thing—
Emilia: Ha?
Iago: To have a foolish wife.
Emilia: O, is that all? What will you give me now   305
  For that same handkerchief?
Iago: What handkerchief?
Emilia: What handkerchief!
  Why, that the Moor first gave to Desdemona;
  That which so often you did bid me steal.
Iago: Hast stol'n it from her?   310
Emilia: No, faith; she let it drop by negligence,
  And to the advantage, I, being here, took't up.
  Look, here it is.
Iago: A good wench; give it me.
Emilia: What will you do with't, that you have been so earnest
  To have me filch it?
Iago: [*Snatching it.*]   Why, what's that to you?   315
Emilia: If it be not for some purpose of import,

319   *Be not acknown on't:* Do not admit to knowing about it; do not acknowledge that you have anything to do with it.

326   *conceits:* ideas or images
326–327 *are in their natures ... distaste:* at first barely cause disgust or seem distasteful
328   *with ... act:* with a little time, (they) have an effect
329   *the mines of sulphur:* Sulphur mines, once on fire, are very difficult to extinguish and seem unquenchable. *I did say so:* apparently Othello's distraught appearance confirms Iago's remarks.
330   *poppy:* opium; *mandragora:* the juice of the mandrake plant, which is a narcotic that induces sleep
331   *drowsy:* inducing sleep
333   *owedst:* possessed or experienced

335   *Avaunt:* away or be off; used to frighten off evil spirits and witches; *on the rack:* a device used for torture that literally tore the body apart at the joints
336   *abused:* wronged or deceived

342   *wanting:* missing

345   *the general camp:* the entire army
346   *Pioners:* pioneers, the soldiers of the lowest status in the army who carried spades and other tools to dig trenches
347   *So:* as long as

Give't me again. Poor lady, she'll run mad
When she shall lack it.
Iago: Be not acknown on't, I have use for it
    Go, leave me.   *[Exit Emilia.]*   320
    I will in Cassio's lodging lose this napkin
    And let him find it. Trifles light as air
    Are to the jealous confirmations strong
    As proofs of holy writ. This may do something.
    The Moor already changes with my poison: 325
    Dangerous conceits are in their natures poisons,
    Which at the first are scarce found to distaste,
    But with a little act upon the blood
    Burn like the mines of sulphur.

    [Enter Othello.]

                          I did say so.
    Look where he comes! Not poppy nor mandragora,   330
    Nor all the drowsy syrups of the world,
    Shall ever medicine thee to that sweet sleep
    Which thou owedst yesterday.
Othello: Ha! ha! false to me?
Iago: Why, how now, general? No more of that.
Othello: Avaunt! Be gone! Thou has set me on the rack.   335
    I swear 'tis better to be much abused
    Than but to know't a little.
Iago: How now, my lord?
Othello: What sense had I of her stol'n hours of lust?
    I saw't not, thought it not, it harm'd not me;
    I slept the next night well, was free and merry;   340
    I found not Cassio's kisses on her lips.
    He that is robb'd, not wanting what is stol'n,
    Let him not know't, and he's not robb'd at all.
Iago: I am sorry to hear this.
Othello: I had been happy if the general camp,   345
    Pioners and all, had tasted her sweet body,
    So I had nothing known. O, now for ever
    Farewell the tranquil mind! farewell content!

349	*plumed:* wearing plumes on their helmets
351	*trump:* trumpet
353	*royal:* splendid or magnificent; *all quality:* all the ranks
354	*Pride, pomp and circumstance...war,* the pageantry or ceremony and accessories of glorious war
355	*mortal engines:* likely cannons; mortal means deadly
356	*The immortal Jove's dread ... counterfeit:* imitate the sound of thunder from the thunderbolts hurled by Jove, the king of the Roman gods
363	*answer:* have to answer to or defend yourself against
365	*probation:* proof—that the proof allows no support to attach a doubt to. In other words, the proof must be so certain that doubts will not change it.
369	*remorse:* repentance or regret because it is not possible to gain forgiveness for what you have done
370	*On ... accumulate:* mount horrors on top of the horror you have already committed
371	*amazed:* paralyzed with horror
373	*that:* the slander against Desdemona and his own torture
375	*God be wi' you:* literally, God be with you, but in the sense of "God help you because I can't"
376	*vice:* failing or shortcoming
379	*profit:* profitable lesson
380	*sith:* since
381	*Nay, stay:* Likely, Othello is calling Iago back. *shouldst be honest:* ought to be honest, to tell the truth
383	*that:* that which

Farewell the plumed troop, and the big wars
That make ambition virtue! O, farewell!   350
Farewell the neighing steed and the shrill trump,
The spirit-stirring drum, the ear-piercing fife,
The royal banner, and all quality,
Pride, pomp, and circumstance of glorious war!
And O, you mortal engines, whose rude throats   355
The immortal Jove's dread clamours counterfeit,
Farewell! Othello's occupation's gone!
Iago: Is't possible, my lord?
Othello: Villain, be sure thou prove my love a whore!
  Be sure of it; give me the ocular proof;   360
  Or, by the worth of man's eternal soul,
  Thou hadst been better have been born a dog
  Than answer my waked wrath!
Iago: Is't come to this?
Othello: Make me to see't; or at the least so prove it
  That the probation bear no hinge nor loop   365
  To hang a doubt on; or woe upon thy life!
Iago: My noble lord—
Othello: If thou dost slander her and torture me,
  Never pray more; abandon all remorse;
  On horror's head horrors accumulate;   370
  Do deeds to make heaven weep, all earth amazed;
  For nothing canst thou to damnation add
  Greater than that.
Iago: O grace! O heaven forgive me!
  Are you a man? Have you a soul or sense?
  God be wi' you! Take mine office. O wretched fool,   375
  That livest to make thine honesty a vice!
  O monstrous world! Take note, take note, O world,
  To be direct and honest is not safe.
  I thank you for this profit; and from hence
  I'll love no friend, sith love breeds such offence.   380
Othello: Nay, stay. Thou shouldst be honest.
Iago: I should be wise; for honesty's a fool
  And loses that it works for.

384   *honest:* pure

387   *Dian's:* referring to the goddess of chastity

390   *Would:* if only

392   *I put it to you:* raised the question with you of Desdemona's infidelity

395   *supervisor:* spectator or one who looks on
396   *topp'd:* from "tupped," a term describing the mating of a ram and a ewe; literally, "covered in cotton"

399   *bolster:* lie together or copulate. A bolster is a long pillow, so the word suggests lying on the same bolster, or perhaps "balter," "to tumble about." The implication is quite clear either way.
400   *More:* other
403   *prime, hot:* full of lust or sexual heat
404   *As ... pride:* as full of lust as wolves in heat

406   *If ... circumstances:* a charge based on circumstantial evidence

410   *office:* duty

412   *Prick'd:* spurred on or urged (as a beast would be)

Othello: By the world,
  I think my wife be honest, and think she is not;
  I think that thou are just, and think thou art not.   385
  I'll have some proof. Her name, that was as fresh
  As Dian's visage, is now begrimed and black
  As mine own face. If there be cords, or knives,
  Poison, or fire, or suffocating streams,
  I'll not endure it. Would I were satisfied!   390
Iago: I see, sir, you are eaten up with passion:
  I do repent me that I put it to you.
  You would be satisfied?
Othello: Would? Nay, I will.
Iago: And may; but how? how satisfied, my lord?
  Would you, the supervisor, grossly gape on?   395
  Behold her topp'd?
Othello: Death and damnation! O!
Iago: It were a tedious difficulty, I think.
  To bring them to that prospect. Damn them then,
  If ever mortal eyes do see them bolster
  More than their own! What then? How then?   400
  What shall I say? Where's satisfaction?
  It is impossible you should see this,
  Were they as prime as goats, as hot as monkeys,
  As salt as wolves in pride, and fools as gross
  As ignorance made drunk. But yet, I say,   405
  If imputation and strong circumstances
  Which lead directly to the door of truth
  Will give you satisfaction, you may have't.
Othello: Give me a living reason she's disloyal.
Iago: I do not like the office.   410
  But sith I am enter'd in this cause so far,
  Prick'd to't by foolish honesty and love,
  I will go on. I lay with Cassio lately,
  And, being troubled with a raging tooth,
  I could not sleep.   415
  There are a kind of men so loose of soul
  That in their sleeps will mutter their affairs.

421   *gripe:* grip

427   *but:* only
428   *denoted ... conclusion:* pointed to something that had
       already happened; a previous experience
429   *shrewd doubt:* strong suspicion

432   *Yet:* up to this point

435   *Spotted ... strawberries:* ornamented or decorated with a
       strawberry pattern

442   *the slave:* a term of contempt likely in reference to Cassio

445   *fond:* foolish

448   *hearted throne:* throne fixed in the heart
449   *fraught:* burden or cargo
450   *aspics' tongues:* refers to small poisonous snakes. Aspics
       are asps, which are found in Egypt and Libya. Othello's
       image is of his heart filled with poison, causing his chest to
       fill with hate.

One of this kind is Cassio.
In sleep I heard him say, "Sweet Desdemona,
Let us be wary, let us hide our loves." 420
And then, sir, would he gripe and wring my hand,
Cry "O sweet creature!" and then kiss me hard,
As if he pluck'd up kisses by the roots
That grew upon my lips; then laid his leg
Over my thigh, and sigh'd, and kiss'd, and then 425
Cried "Cursed fate that gave thee to the Moor!"
Othello: O monstrous! monstrous!
Iago: Nay, this was but his dream.
Othello: But this denoted a foregone conclusion:
'Tis a shrewd doubt, though it be but a dream.
Iago: And this may help to thicken other proofs 430
That do demonstrate thinly.
Othello: I'll tear her all to pieces.
Iago: Nay, but be wise. Yet we see nothing done;
She may be honest yet. Tell me but this:
Have you not sometimes seen a handkerchief
Spotted with strawberries in your wife's hand? 435
Othello: I gave her such a one; 'twas my first gift.
Iago: I know not that; but such a handkerchief—
I am sure it was your wife's—did I to-day
See Cassio wipe his beard with.
Othello: If it be that—
Iago: If it be that, or any that was hers, 440
It speaks against her with the other proofs.
Othello: O, that the slave had forty thousand lives!
One is too poor, too weak for my revenge.
Now do I see 'tis true. Look here, Iago;
All my fond love thus do I blow to heaven. 445
'Tis gone.
Arise, black vengeance, from thy hollow cell!
Yield up, O love, thy crown and hearted throne
To tyrannous hate! Swell, bosom, with thy fraught,
For 'tis of aspics' tongues!
Iago: Yet be content. 450

453–456   *the Pontic sea ... Hellespont:* The Pontic sea is the Black
          Sea, which empties into the sea of Marmora (the Propontic)
          and through the Dardanelles (the Hellespont) to the
          Mediterranean. The water flowing into the Black Sea comes
          from a deep current, and this outward flow is constant
          because of it. *compulsive:* caused by compulsion, com-
          pelled; *due:* straight, properly or by necessity

459   *capable:* full

460   *marble heaven:* the streaked sky, or possibly cold and
          unfeeling

462   *engage:* pledge

464   *clip:* surround

465–466   *give up ... wit:* give up the use or the working of his
          intelligence

468–469   *remorse ... ever:* an obligation regardless of how bloody the
          business

470   *bounteous:* wholehearted

471   *put thee to't:* put you to the test or task

475   *minx:* whore or loose woman

Othello: O, blood, blood, blood!
Iago: Patience, I say. Your mind perhaps may change.
Othello: Never, Iago. Like to the Pontic sea,
    Whose icy current and compulsive course
    Ne'er feels retiring ebb, but keeps due on   455
    To the Propontic and the Hellespont,
    Even so my bloody thoughts, with violent pace,
    Shall ne'er look back, ne'er ebb to humble love,
    Till that a capable and wide revenge
    Swallow them up. Now, by yond marble heaven,   460
    In the due reverence of a sacred vow   [*Kneels.*]
    I here engage my words.
Iago: Do not rise yet.   [*Iago kneels.*]
    Witness, you ever-burning lights above,
    You elements that clip us round about,
    Witness that here Iago doth give up   465
    The execution of his wit, hands, heart
    To wrong'd Othello's service! Let him command,
    And to obey shall be in me remorse,
    What bloody business ever.   [*They rise.*]
Othello: I greet thy love,
    Not with vain thanks but with acceptance bounteous.   470
    And will upon the instant put thee to't.
    Within these three days let me hear thee say
    That Cassio's not alive.
Iago: My friend is dead; 'tis done at your request.
    But let her live.
Othello: Damn her, lewd minx! O, damn her!   475
    Come, go with me apart. I will withdraw
    To furnish me with some swift means of death
    For the fair devil. Now art thou my lieutenant.
Iago: I am your own for ever.   [*Exeunt.*]

Act 3, Scene 3: Activities

1. In a journal entry, decide to what extent you feel you can rely on other people to act in ways that you expect them to.

2. In this scene, Desdemona seems to be guaranteeing things to Cassio she really has no business guaranteeing. Discuss with your group why she thinks she can do this. What makes her so certain that Othello will agree to what she is asking? If you were in the role of Desdemona, how would you convince an audience that you were genuine? Write this as an explanation of how you see your role.

3. You are the owner of a pub in Cyprus. You are having a conversation with a regular customer about the sudden influx of Venetians into your area. Record the conversation that indicates what the two of you think about this recent deployment of military personnel into your area, and try to explain what you think is going on. What might be the advantages and disadvantages of these developments from your perspective?

4. In this scene, Othello says to Desdemona, "When I love thee not, chaos is come again" (lines 91–92). Those are rather profound words.

   a) Discuss with your group how we might express this sentiment today. Consider how you regard such statements: are they dangerous oversimplifications or just expressions of blind love?

   OR

   b) Statements such as these can sometimes come back to haunt us. Record in your journal situations you know about where people who have said such things have been disappointed in the end. Many television programs and movies include such a plot. In your opinion, how might this happen to Othello? Create a soliloquy for Othello that might logically fit into the play at this point.

5. With a partner, outline the argument that Iago uses to completely change Othello's thoughts from absolute love to

distrust. Based on your own media experiences, determine how plausible this scenario might be. Write your own soap-opera script using what you have discovered here. Who are your characters and what makes them come alive? What story are you trying to tell?

6. Iago says to Othello, "Men should be what they seem" (line 126).

   a) How dangerous might it be to operate on such an assumption? In your experience, does this statement hold true? Write your thoughts in your journal.

   b) Write a short poem about Iago, using this line as a beginning. Or write an essay using examples of famous historical characters who did not live up to the statement at all. Have you ever made a similar statement yourself?

7. In lines 260–277, Othello talks about marriage, using the strangest images. The metaphor of his speech centres around hawks and hunting. Read the speech again and draw a picture that would illustrate the metaphor he uses. Find a key line to use as a caption for your illustration. Do you agree with Othello's metaphor?

8. An often quoted line is Iago's "Who steals my purse steals trash; 'tis something, nothing" (line 157). Out of context, this could mean almost anything. Give your interpretation of this line. In the context of the scene, what is its function? Does this differ from your original thoughts about it? What is Iago doing here, anyway? A group discussion could help clarify your thoughts and help you understand how manipulation works. What is the basis of Iago's argument and how successful is it? What do you think about doing that kind of thing?

9. Othello's question, "Think'st thou I'd make a life of jealousy...?" (line 177) may reveal many things about his character. Discuss with your group what you think these things are. Write your own analysis of Othello at this point using the information and opinions raised in your discussion. What is your own opinion about jealousy?

10. As you have probably noted, there are many symbols used by the characters in this play when they are passionate

about something. We all use symbols in this way. What symbols would you create to represent the following: honesty, dishonesty, honour, anger, love, hate, war, peace, deception, good, and evil? Choose four of these and apply them to a character you think each fits. You can display your final versions on chart paper (or the blackboard) for the rest of the class to see and comment on. You might try a quiz in which you take turns guessing who is who by their "symbol-map" alone!

11. The handkerchief incident is generally considered to be a key one in the play. Do you agree? Why would anyone be obsessed with a decorated handkerchief? It obviously meant something to Othello. Given Othello's background, what do you think its significance was? Emilia seems to recognize its importance, so why doesn't she return it to Desdemona immediately? In your group, discuss and interpret this strange sequence of events. Can anybody trust anybody in this play? Can you trust your friends? Write a 300-word article for a magazine in which you use this incident as the centre for your observations about trust.

12. At this point, how much does Othello really know about Desdemona? Does he understand the Venetian background she came from? How much does Desdemona know about Othello? In your opinion, was this a wise marriage? As a counsellor, what might you have said to both Desdemona and Othello had you been able to talk to them before they were married? In your journal, record your observations about where this relationship might be going, or discuss it with your group before you share your observations with the class.

13. How would you, as a director, shoot this "handkerchief" scene? With your group, plan, sketch, and perform your version of how this might be accomplished without it appearing silly. You might first want to answer the question about Emilia's motives. Does she have any? What extra information might the "handkerchief incident" give you about Emilia? Write a profile of her from this perspective.

14. Suddenly, Othello feels he was tricked and deceived. He goes into a rant (lines 338–357). What is he talking about? What does he mean by his outburst, "Othello's occupation's gone"? How does Iago take advantage of this situation? Discuss with your group some different ways of rendering these key speeches. Decide on a version you prefer, and write a director's note explaining exactly how you want the speeches delivered. You might even wish to rehearse some of the ideas your group comes up with to test their impact and effectiveness.

15. In lines 453–462, Othello firmly states that he will never change his mind about his decision, and he uses a simile referring to the Pontic Sea, the Propontic and the Hellespont. Locate these places on the map on page ii and then explain the simile to a partner. In your opinion, is this comparison effective? Why doesn't Othello simply say, "Once I make up my mind, nothing can change it"?

16. Does it appear to you that Iago wants Desdemona dead? How would you justify that opinion? Write your thoughts in your journal.

17. What do you think are the most significant events in this scene? Prepare your own brief summary of it in the fewest words possible. What picture comes into your mind? Sketch it.

For the next scene ...

From your reading and viewing experience, would you agree that even the most sympathetic characters often lie to or deceive themselves or others? Why do they do this? Do they know what they are doing?

Act 3, Scene 4

In this scene ...

Desdemona, unaware of what is going on, persists in trying to have Cassio reinstated. We learn that she is concerned about the loss of her handkerchief because she fears that Othello might be upset at its disappearance. Her anxiety intensifies when Othello asks her for it and is quite angry when she cannot produce it. Cassio and Iago enter. Iago insists that Cassio's only hope is to ask Desdemona to help, so Cassio once again entreats Desdemona to use her influence with her husband on his behalf. But Desdemona tells him that Othello seems distraught, at which Iago pretends concern and decides to find him. Desdemona and Emilia also leave, and Bianca, Cassio's mistress, enters. Cassio gives Bianca Desdemona's handkerchief, explaining that he found it in his room and asking her to reproduce the embroidery for him. This, of course, makes Bianca jealous even though Cassio denies any involvement with another woman.

1   *sirrah:* a term of address used for servants or social inferiors;
                 lies: lives

4   *is stabbing:* is cause to be stabbed
5   *Go to:* an expression of impatience, similar to "come on!"

9–10   *lie in mine own throat:* the clown puns on the word "lie"

11   *edified:* enlightened or instructed

14   *moved:* successfully urged or appealed to

16   *compass:* limits or range

18   *should I lose:* could I have lost

21   *crusadoes:* Portuguese gold coins with the figure of the
                 cross on them

26   *humours:* moods believed to be connected to the bodily
                 fluids

Scene 4

Before the castle.
Enter Desdemona, Emilia, and Clown.

Desdemona: Do you know, sirrah, where Lieutenant Cassio lies?
Clown: I dare not say he lies anywhere.
Desdemona: Why, man?
Clown: He's a soldier, and for me to say a soldier lies is stabbing.
Desdemona: Go to. Where lodges he? 5
Clown: To tell you where he lodges is to tell you where I lie.
Desdemona: Can anything be made of this?
Clown: I know not where he lodges; and for me to devise a
lodging, and say he lies here or he lies there, were to lie in
mine own throat. 10
Desdemona: Can you enquire him out, and be edified by report?
Clown: I will catechize the world for him; that is, make questions,
and by them answer.
Desdemona: Seek him, bid him come hither. Tell him I have moved
my lord on his behalf and hope all will be well. 15
Clown: To do this is within the compass of man's wit, and
therefore I will attempt the doing of it.   [*Exit.*]
Desdemona: Where should I lose that handkerchief, Emilia?
Emilia: I know not, madam.
Desdemona: Believe me, I had rather have lost my purse 20
Full of crusadoes; and but my noble Moor
Is true of mind, and made of no such baseness
As jealous creatures are, it were enough
To put him to ill thinking.
Emilia: Is he not jealous?
Desdemona: Who? He? I think the sun where he was born 25
Drew all such humours from him.
Emilia: Look where he comes.

29   *hardness to dissemble:* How difficult it is to lie!

31   *moist:* A hot palm was thought to indicate a passionate and amorous nature.

33   *liberal:* generous

35   *sequester:* separation

36   *castigation:* corrective punishment; *exercise devout:* religious acts of devotion

41–42   *the hearts ... not hearts:* In earlier times, love and deeds went together, but now it is deeds of faithlessness that prevail ("hands that liberally give away hearts").

44   *chuck:* a term of endearment

45   *sent:* a messenger

46   *a salt ... rheum:* troublesome head cold; *offends:* bothers

52   *charmer:* a witch; someone who uses charms and spells

53   *She:* the charmer; *her, she:* my mother

54   *amiable:* desirable, lovable

[*Enter Othello.*]

Desdemona: I will not leave him now till Cassio
 Be call'd to him.—How is't with you, my lord?
Othello: Well, my good lady. [*Aside.*] O, hardness to dissemble!
 How do you, Desdemona?
Desdemona: Well, my good lord.   30
Othello: Give me your hand. This hand is moist, my lady.
Desdemona: It yet hath felt no age nor known no sorrow.
Othello: This argues fruitfulness and liberal heart.
 Hot, hot, and moist. This hand of yours requires
 A sequester from liberty, fasting and prayer,   35
 Much castigation, exercise devout;
 For here's a young and sweating devil here
 That commonly rebels. 'Tis a good hand,
 A frank one.
Desdemona: You may, indeed, say so;
 For 'twas that hand that gave away my heart.   40
Othello: A liberal hand: the hearts of old gave hands;
 But our new heraldry is hands, not hearts.
Desdemona: I cannot speak of this. Come now, your promise!
Othello: What promise, chuck?
Desdemona: I have sent to bid Cassio come speak with you.   45
Othello: I have a salt and sorry rheum offends me.
 Lend me thy handkerchief.
Desdemona: Here, my lord.
Othello: That which I gave you.
Desdemona: I have it not about me.
Othello: Not?
Desdemona: No, faith, my lord.
Othello: That is a fault.
 That handkerchief   50
 Did an Egyptian to my mother give.
 She was a charmer, and could almost read
 The thoughts of people. She told her, while she kept it,
 'Twould make her amiable and subdue my father
 Entirely to her love; but if she lost it   55

57	*hold her:* regard her as
58	*fancies:* loves
60	*her:* my wife; *take heed on't:* take care of it, pay attention to it
61	*Make it a darling:* value it
62	*perdition:* disaster, ruin
64	*web:* woven fabric
65–66	*A sibyl ... compasses:* a prophetess who is two hundred years old; *course:* travel; *compasses:* annual circuits
67	*fury:* inspired frenzy
69	*mummy:* a drug made from the balsamic liquid running from mummified bodies, thought to have medicinal power especially in terms of epilepsy
70	*Conserved:* preserved or made from
72	*would:* I wish
73	*Wherefore:* why
74	*startlingly:* urgently, in stops and starts or in irregular spells; *rash:* urgently, hastily
75	*out o' the way:* lost or missing
78	*an if:* if
82	*suit:* petition
86	*sufficient:* capable

Or made a gift of it, my father's eye
Should hold her loathed, and his spirits should hunt
After new fancies. She, dying, gave it me,
And bid me, when my fate would have me wive,
To give it her. I did so; and take heed on't; 60
Make it a darling like your precious eye.
To lose't or give't away were such perdition
As nothing else could match.
Desdemona: Is't possible?
Othello: 'Tis true. There's magic in the web of it.
A sibyl that had number'd in the world 65
The sun to course two hundred compasses,
In her prophetic fury sew'd the work;
The worms were hallow'd that did breed the silk;
And it was dyed in mummy which the skilful
Conserved of maidens' hearts.
Desdemona: Indeed? Is't true? 70
Othello: Most veritable; therefore look to't well.
Desdemona: Then would to God that I had never seen't!
Othello: Ha! Wherefore?
Desdemona: Why do you speak so startingly and rash?
Othello: Is't lost? Is't gone? Speak, is it out o' the way? 75
Desdemona: Heaven bless us!
Othello: Say you?
Desdemona: It is not lost. But what an if it were?
Othello: How?
Desdemona: I say it is not lost.
Othello: Fetch't, let me see't! 80
Desdemona: Why, so I can, sir; but I will not now.
This is a trick to put me from my suit;
Pray you let Cassio be received again.
Othello: Fetch me the handkerchief! My mind misgives.
Desdemona: Come, come! 85
You'll never meet a more sufficient man.
Othello: The handkerchief!
Desdemona: I pray talk me of Cassio.
Othello: The handkerchief!

92   *blame:* at fault or in the wrong (for speaking to me like this)

97   *unhappy:* miserable

98   *'Tis not ... man:* It doesn't take more than a year or two to know what a man is really like.

99   *are all but:* are nothing but

100   *hungerly:* hungrily or greedily

101   *belch:* vomit

103   *happiness:* lucky chance; *importune:* beg urgently or persistently

108   *office:* duty

109   *would not be:* do not want to be

110   *mortal:* fatal or deadly

111   *nor ... sorrows:* neither my military service in the past nor my regrets now for misbehaving

112   *Nor ... futurity:* good resolves for the future

114–117   *But ... alms:* If Othello will not restore me to favour, I shall at least benefit by forcing myself to be content and to restrict the search for my fortune elsewhere, or perhaps to take what gifts fortune gives me.

118   *advocation:* pleading on your behalf

120   *favour:* appearance

Desdemona: A man that all his time
  Hath founded his good fortunes on your love,
  Shared dangers with you— 90
Othello: The handkerchief!
Desdemona: In sooth you are to blame.
Othello: Away! [*Exit.*]
Emilia: Is not this man jealous?
Desdemona: I ne'er saw this before. 95
  Sure there's some wonder in this handkerchief;
  I am most unhappy in the loss of it.
Emilia: 'Tis not a year or two shows us a man.
  They are all but stomachs, and we all but food;
  They eat us hungerly, and when they are full, 100
  They belch us.

  [*Enter Iago and Cassio.*]

  Look you, Cassio and my husband.
Iago: There is no other way; 'tis she must do't.
  And lo the happiness! Go and importune her.
Desdemona: How now, good Cassio? What's the news with you?
Cassio: Madam, my former suit. I do beseech you 105
  That by your virtuous means I may again
  Exist, and be a member of his love
  Whom I with all the office of my heart
  Entirely honour. I would not be delay'd.
  If my offence be of such mortal kind 110
  That nor my service past, nor present sorrows,
  Nor purposed merit in futurity,
  Can ransom me into his love again,
  But to know so must be my benefit.
  So shall I clothe me in a forced content, 115
  And shut myself up in some other course,
  To fortune's alms.
Desdemona: Alas, thrice-gentle Cassio!
  My advocation is not now in tune.
  My lord is not my lord; nor should I know him,
  Were he in favour as in humour alter'd. 120

123	*stood ... blank:* The blank is the white spot in the centre of an archery target, thus, becomes the target of his displeasure.
124	*free:* frank, open, unreserved
128	*unquietness:* unease or upset
135	*Something ... state:* surely some affair of state (public business)
136	*unhatch'd practice:* undisclosed plot
137	*Made demonstrable:* revealed
138	*puddled:* muddied or muddled
140	*object:* those that really concern them
141–143	*let our ... pain:* When our finger aches it makes the rest of the body hurt as well.
143–145	*Nay, we must ... bridal:* We must not expect men to pay as much attention to things other than their work, such as a honeymoon.
145	*Beshrew me:* evil fall upon me or curse me
146	*unhandsome:* unskilled or clumsy
147	*Arraigning ... soul:* accusing him of being unkind or of exhibiting unnatural conduct; *with my soul:* from my heart and soul
148	*suborn'd the witness:* corrupted the witness (herself)
149	*he's indicted:* Othello is convicted
151	*toy:* a silly notion or trifle

So help me every spirit sanctified
As I have spoken for you all my best
And stood within the blank of his displeasure
For my free speech! You must awhile be patient.
What I can do I will; and more I will   125
Than for myself I dare. Let that suffice you.
Iago: Is my lord angry?
Emilia: He went hence but now,
   And certainly in strange unquietness.
Iago: Can he be angry? I have seen the cannon
   When it hath blown his ranks into the air   130
   And, like the devil, from his very arm
   Puff'd his own brother; and can he be angry?
   Something of moment then. I will go meet him.
   There's matter in't indeed if he be angry.
Desdemona: I prithee, do so.   [*Exit Iago.*]
                                    Something sure of state,   135
   Either from Venice or some unhatch'd practice
   Made demonstrable here in Cyprus to him,
   Hath puddled his clear spirit; and in such cases
   Men's natures wrangle with inferior things,
   Though great ones are their object. 'Tis even so;   140
   For let our finger ache, and it endues
   Our other healthful members even to that sense
   Of pain. Nay, we must think men are not gods,
   Nor of them look for such observancy
   As fits the bridal. Beshrew me much, Emilia,   145
   I was, unhandsome warrior as I am,
   Arraigning his unkindness with my soul;
   But now I find I had suborn'd the witness,
   And he's indicted falsely.
Emilia: Pray heaven it be state-matters, as you think,   150
   And no conception nor no jealous toy
   Concerning you.
Desdemona: Alas the day, I never gave him cause.
Emilia: But jealous souls will not be answer'd so;
   They are not ever jealous for the cause,   155

156 *for:* because

157 *Begot:* conceived

161 *fit:* receptive, willing to listen

164 *What ... home:* What are you doing away from home?

169 *Eight ... hours:* seven days and nights

169–170 *lovers' absent hours ... times:* An hour of a lover's absence is 160 times more tiresome and tedious than all the hours on a clock's dial.

172 *press'd:* weighed down

173 *more continuate:* long continued or less interrupted

174 *Strike ... absence:* pay off my debt of absence so it can be cancelled; *score:* a debt originally marked on a post by scoring (cutting) it with notches

175 *Take ... out:* Copy this embroidery for me in another hand-kerchief.

181 *remembrance:* keepsake

184 *ere it be demanded:* before its owner asks for it back

But jealous for they are jealous. 'Tis a monster
Begot upon itself, born on itself.
Desdemona: Heaven keep that monster from Othello's mind!
Emilia: Lady, amen.
Desdemona: I will go seek him. Cassio, walk here about: 160
  If I do find him fit, I'll move your suit
  And seek to effect it to my uttermost.
Cassio: I humbly thank your ladyship.
                                [*Exeunt Desdemona and Emilia.*]

  [*Enter Bianca.*]

Bianca: Save you, friend Cassio!
Cassio: What make you from home?
  How is it with you, my most fair Bianca?   165
  I' faith, sweet love, I was coming to your house.
Bianca: And I was going to your lodging, Cassio.
  What, keep a week away? seven days and nights?
  Eight score eight hours? and lovers' absent hours,
  More tedious than the dial eight score times?   170
  O weary reckoning!
Cassio: Pardon me, Bianca:
  I have this while with leaden thoughts been press'd;
  But I shall in a more continuate time
  Strike off this score of absence. Sweet Bianca,
           [*Giving her Desdemona's handkerchief.*]
  Take me this work out.
Bianca: O Cassio, whence came this?   175
  This is some token from a newer friend.
  To the felt absence now I feel a cause.
  Is't come to this? Well, well.
Cassio: Go to, woman!
  Throw your vile guesses in the devil's teeth,
  From whence you have them. You are jealous now   180
  That this is from some mistress, some remembrance.
  No, by my faith, Bianca.
Bianca: Why, whose is it?
Cassio: I know not, sweet; I found it in my chamber.
  I like the work well; ere it be demanded,

188   *attend here on:* wait for
189   *addition:* advantage or possibly credit
190   *woman'd:* burdened with a woman

192   *bring me:* go with me
193   *at night:* tonight

196   *circumstanced:* surrounded by or governed by conditions;
        accept your terms and conditions

As like enough it will, I'ld have it copied.   185
    Take it and do't, and leave me for this time.
Bianca: Leave you? Wherefore?
Cassio: I do attend here on the general
    And think it no addition, nor my wish,
    To have him see me woman'd.
Bianca: Why, I pray you?   190
Cassio: Not that I love you not.
Bianca: But that you do not love me.
    I pray you bring me on the way a little,
    And say if I shall see you soon at night.
Cassio: 'Tis but a little way that I can bring you,
    For I attend here; but I'll see you soon.   195
Bianca: 'Tis very good. I must be circumstanced.   [*Exeunt.*]

Act 3, Scene 4: Activities

1. The stage directions for this scene say "Before the castle." With your group, design a set that would give this scene a sense of "place" or location. You will have to consider what happens in the scene to do this, and you might want to consider the images the speeches create to help reinforce what you think the thrust or theme of this scene should be.

2. Desdemona seems to be frantic about the loss of her handkerchief. Discuss with your group what this might indicate about the state of her marriage. Could she not explain to Othello that she simply lost it? Do you have anything that you prize as a memento that you would be upset about losing? Why do people attach so much value to such things? You might wish to write a personal account in your journal describing an experience of your own.

3. Desdemona does not seem to understand Othello's sudden change of mood and attitude. Othello aggravates her anxiety by saying about the handkerchief, "there's magic in the web of it." As Desdemona, write a diary entry that explores your feelings about the relationship between this handkerchief, your marriage, and your future dealings with your husband.

4. Select several key lines from Desdemona's speeches, or paraphrase her dialogue up to this point. Use these to create a monologue for her that conveys your impression of her character in this scene.

5. In lines 98–101, Emilia says some unflattering things about men in general. Write a response to her, perhaps as a letter, either agreeing with her assessment or arguing against it. Base your responses only on the behaviour of the characters in the play. Share your responses with others for their reaction.

6. Desdemona now sees a side of Othello she did not know existed. With a partner, discuss what effect it seems to have on her and how she deals with it. Emilia doesn't seem to be of much help. Add a speech for her in which she makes more of an attempt to console Desdemona.

7. This scene shows us in a very objective way the results of Iago's plotting. He does not say very much himself in this scene, but he sees that things are working perfectly for him. Write an aside, a soliloquy, or a monologue in which he makes clear how pleased he is with himself.

8. Why doesn't Othello simply ask Desdemona if she has been unfaithful? Today, they might seek marital counselling. What do you suppose a counsellor might say to the two of them in a session? How likely do you think they would be to follow any advice offered, knowing what you do about both of them? Write your assessment as a report.

9. From what you can gather from the play, recreate Othello's past. What might this explain about his ability to seduce Desdemona by merely talking to her? Why is he so quick to jealousy? How would you feel in the presence of this man?

Act 3: Consider the Whole Act

1. This act highlights two central themes of the play: deceit and jealousy. Even the sympathetic characters display aspects of each by deceiving themselves or others, although they are less conscious of their behaviour than Iago is of his. How does this happen? In your opinion, is this a common form of behaviour among people under stress? Relate an incident you know about in which a person used deceit to get what he or she wanted. What was the outcome? How does a person avoid falling into this trap?

2. Love triangles are a source for many story plots, including this one. Is there more than one here? What purpose do such plots serve? The triangle involving Roderigo seems to exist mostly in his own mind, but along with the one involving Cassio that exists in Iago's mind, these become something other than ludicrous parodies and turn into something genuinely menacing. How does this come about? How could any of these plots have been resolved before they became dangerous?

3. With your group, select a character from the play, and have each member write two statements about that person on separate cards. Collect all the cards and exchange them with another group who has done a different character. Shuffle the cards and come up with five statements that you all agree with, and use these to write a profile of that character. Compare your group profile with the others in the class, presuming each group has chosen or agreed to work on a different character. Look at the cards you rejected and decide why you found them unacceptable.

4. More than one character is to blame for the events unfolding as they have so far. Make a list of these characters and decide how each has contributed to the difficulties depicted in Act 3. Try to determine what their true motivations were.

5. Write a short research paper on some aspect of Act 3 that especially interests you. You could visit Web sites that contain current articles on *Othello* and use the information there. You can post your completed paper on the bulletin board to share with the rest of the class, or you might use your research as the basis for a magazine article that explores the problem beyond the play itself.

6. There are reasons contained in the text itself that suggest why Othello and Desdemona's marriage has reached the stage of mistrust depicted in Act 3. To determine what happened, consider the following:

   • Othello's background as a soldier. How long has he been in the military?
   • What first-hand knowledge of Venetian society does Othello have?
   • What does he know about functioning in a peacetime society?
   • What does he know about Venetian women, and from whom does he learn it? What kind of information does he get?
   • What does Othello know of Venetian culture and its customs, and how does he learn that? Who gives him advice about it?

- What seems to be Othello's dominant characteristic? How would you explain that?
- Are the traits of a good soldier necessarily the same as those of a good husband?
- What is the age difference between Desdemona and Othello? Does this matter? Does colour matter? Do background differences matter?
- What kind of life did Desdemona have when growing up?
- What might be the effect of suddenly moving to Cyprus immediately after the marriage?
- Do the two have any common ground at all? Are there signs that the two may be dependent on each other?

What other questions come to mind?

As you answer the above questions and factor Iago into the equation, what kind of picture emerges? In your opinion, what is the value of looking at the play from this perspective?

For the next scene ...

It is generally agreed that reason and emotion have to be kept in balance. What happens when emotion takes over a person? Recall an incident when you have seen this happen. What was the result? How easy is it to "reason" with a person who is overcome by emotion?

Act 4, Scene 1

In this scene ...

Iago continues to provoke and torment Othello with graphic descriptions of Desdemona's infidelities until he has him believing that Cassio actually bragged about their love affair. Othello is so distraught and overcome that he faints. Cassio enters and wants to revive him, but Iago persuades him to leave and return when the trance has run its course. Othello revives, and Iago reminds him that many wives are unfaithful to their husbands. He advises Othello to conceal himself so that he can see and overhear a conversation between Cassio and Iago. Cassio returns, and watching from his hiding place, Othello believes that Cassio is boasting about his torrid affair with Desdemona. Cassio is, of course, talking about Bianca. Othello's rage grows. At this point, Bianca herself arrives and accuses Cassio of having received the handkerchief he gave her from "some minx." Othello sees the handkerchief in Bianca's hands and assumes Cassio has passed Desdemona's gift along to his mistress. Bianca storms out in a temper, and Iago convinces Cassio he should follow her. Othello now leaves his hiding place and vows to kill Cassio and poison Desdemona, but Iago suggests that he strangle her in her "contaminated" bed. Othello agrees, and Iago promises to deal with Cassio. Desdemona enters accompanied by Lodovico, a kinsman of her father's from Venice. Lodovico has brought orders from the Duke that Othello return to Venice and that in his place Cassio be placed in command in Cyprus. Suddenly Othello strikes Desdemona, to the horror of the others, then rudely dismisses her, heaping insults on her as she leaves. Lodovico is now convinced—with some help from Iago—that Othello has lost his senses, and follows him to further observe his behaviour.

6   *hypocrisy ... devil:* To appear good while doing evil is hypocrisy against God, so to seem evil while "not meaning any harm" is hypocrisy against the devil. "Against" means in full view of or in front of, with the implication of cheating or deceiving the devil.

8   *they tempt heaven:* test the grace of God to keep them from sin. The idea is that those who sleep together and mean no harm are really asking the devil to tempt them, all the while inviting God's suspicion of their innocence.

9   *So:* as long as; *venial slip:* forgivable fault or pardonable sin

17   *They have... it not:* Probably the sense is that many people are mistakenly credited with having an invisible or immeasurable reputation (essence) for honour.

21   *As doth ... house:* The raven was thought to be a bird of ill omen that hovered over plague-infected houses.

22   *Boding:* predicting in an ominous way (foreboding)

Act 4, Scene 1

Cyprus. Before the castle.
Enter Othello and Iago.

Iago: Will you think so?
Othello: Think so, Iago?
Iago: What,
   To kiss in private?
Othello: An unauthorized kiss.
Iago: Or to be naked with her friend in bed
   An hour or more, not meaning any harm?
Othello: Naked in bed, Iago, and not mean harm!   5
   It is hypocrisy against the devil.
   They that mean virtuously, and yet do so,
   The devil their virtue tempts, and they tempt heaven.
Iago: So they do nothing, 'tis a venial slip.
   But if I give my wife a handkerchief—   10
Othello: What then?
Iago: Why, then 'tis hers, my lord; and being hers,
   She may, I think, bestow't on any man.
Othello: She is protectress of her honour too;
   May she give that?   15
Iago: Her honour is an essence that's not seen;
   They have it very oft that have it not.
   But for the handkerchief—
Othello: By heaven, I would most gladly have forgot it!
   Thou said'st—O, it comes o'er my memory   20
   As doth the raven o'er the infected house,
   Boding to all!—he had my handkerchief.
Iago: Ay, what of that?
Othello: That's not so good now.
Iago: What

26	*importunate:* urgent, pressing
27	*voluntary dotage:* self-induced and foolish affection or infatuation
28	*Convinced ... them:* having overcome their reluctance, or perhaps sexually satisfied them

36	*belie:* lie about; *fulsome:* disgusting or obscene
37–38	*To confess ... hanged:* a proverbial expression meaning "you lie"; literally, "first hang and then hear why it happened"
39	*invest:* clothe
40	*shadowing:* overshadowing, or perhaps even creating images

52	*lethargy:* lapsing into unconsciousness; *his:* its

If I had said I had seen him do you wrong?
Or heard him say—as knaves be such abroad 25
Who having, by their own importunate suit,
Or voluntary dotage of some mistress,
Convinced or supplied them, cannot choose
But they must blab—
Othello: Hath he said anything?
Iago: He hath, my lord; but be you well assured, 30
 No more than he'll unswear.
Othello: What hath he said?
Iago: Faith, that he did—I know not what he did.
Othello: What? what?
Iago: Lie—
Othello: With her?
Iago: With her, on her; what you will.
Othello: Lie with her? lie on her?—We say lie on her when 35
   they belie her.—Lie with her! 'Zounds, that's fulsome.—
   Handkerchief—confessions—handkerchief!—To confess,
   and be hanged for his labour—first to be hanged, and then
   to confess. I tremble at it. Nature would not invest herself
   in such shadowing passion without some instruction. It is 40
   not words that shakes me thus. Pish! Noses, ears, and lips?
   Is't possible?—Confess?—Handkerchief? O devil!
                              [*Falls in a trance.*]
Iago: Work on,
   My medicine, work! Thus credulous fools are caught,
   And many worthy and chaste dames even thus, 45
   All guiltless, meet reproach. What, ho! my lord!
   My lord, I say! Othello.

   [*Enter Cassio.*]

                        How now, Cassio?
Cassio: What's the matter?
Iago: My lord is fall'n into an epilepsy.
   This is his second fit; he had one yesterday. 50
Cassio: Rub him about the temples.
Iago: No, forbear.
   The lethargy must have his quiet course.

53   *by and by:* eventually

56   *straight:* immediately
57   *great occasion:* an important matter or subject

59   *mock me:* This refers to Iago's question about his head, and
            the suggestion is that Othello's head is sprouting the horns
            of the cuckold.
60   *Would:* I wish
61   *horned man:* a cuckold. A cuckold is a horned beast
            (monster).
63   *civil:* civilized

65–66   *every ... you:* The sense is that every married man is poten-
            tially a cuckold because they are like yoked oxen (horned
            beasts) pulling a heavy load, with a play on "yoke" meaning
            also married. "Bearded" implies anyone old enough to grow
            a beard.
67   *unproper beds:* Because the wives have lovers, men's beds
            are never truly their own.
68   *swear peculiar:* are positive are exclusively theirs
70   *lip ... couch:* kiss (perhaps obscenely) an unchaste woman
            in a bed, free from anxiety, fear, or suspicion ("secure
            couch")
74   *Confine ... in a patient list:* keep yourself within the limits of
            patience or order

77   *shifted him away:* got rid of him or got him out of the way
78   *laid ... ecstasy:* provided a believable explanation for your
            fit or state of unconsciousness
79   *anon:* immediately or soon
80   *encave:* hide or conceal
81   *fleers, the gibes:* sneers and unflattering remarks (as in
            making fun of)

85   *cope:* meet, but also copulate with, as in copemate
86   *but ... patience:* Just notice his manner or behaviour, and,
            indeed, be patient or calm.

If not, he foams at mouth, and by and by
Breaks out to savage madness. Look, he stirs.
Do you withdraw yourself a little while,   55
He will recover straight. When he is gone,
I would on great occasion speak with you.   [*Exit Cassio.*]
How is it, general? Have you not hurt your head?
Othello: Dost thou mock me?
Iago: I mock you? No, by heaven.
Would you would bear your fortune like a man!   60
Othello: A horned man's a monster and a beast.
Iago: There's many a beast then in a populous city,
And many a civil monster.
Othello: Did he confess it?
Iago: Good sir, be a man.
Think every bearded fellow that's but yoked   65
May draw with you. There's millions now alive
That nightly lie in those unproper beds
Which they dare swear peculiar: your case is better.
O, 'tis the spite of hell, the fiend's arch-mock,
To lip a wanton in a secure couch,   70
And to suppose her chaste! No, let me know,
And knowing what I am, I know what she shall be.
Othello: O, thou art wise! 'Tis certain.
Iago: Stand you awhile apart;
Confine yourself but in a patient list.
Whilst you were here, o'erwhelmed with your grief—   75
A passion most unsuiting such a man—
Cassio came hither. I shifted him away
And laid good 'scuse upon your ecstasy;
Bade him anon return, and here speak with me;
The which he promised. Do but encave yourself   80
And mark the fleers, the gibes, and notable scorns
That dwell in every region of his face;
For I will make him till the tale anew,
Where, how, how oft, how long ago, and when
He hath, and is again to cope your wife.   85
I say, but mark his gesture. Marry, patience;

87	*all ... spleen:* totally turned into spleen (the source of violent passion or anger)

91	*keep time:* remain in control
92	*of:* about
93	*huswife:* hussy or a prostitute

100	*unbookish:* ignorant; *construe:* interpret
101	*light:* frivolous

103	*worser:* worse; *addition:* the title of lieutenant. Cassio feels worse when Iago reminds him of the title he has lost.
104	*want:* lack

107	*speed:* succeed; *caitiff:* wretch

112	*importunes:* begs persistently
113	*o'er:* over again; *well said:* well done (said sarcastically)

117	*Roman:* probably a reference to the Roman public celebrations (triumph) of victory

Or I shall say you are all in all in spleen,
And nothing of a man.
Othello: Dost thou hear, Iago?
  I will be found most cunning in my patience;
  But—dost thou hear?—most bloody.
Iago: That's not amiss;   90
  But yet keep time in all. Will you withdraw? [*Othello retires.*]
  Now will I question Cassio of Bianca,
  A huswife that by selling her desires
  Buys herself bread and clothes. It is a creature
  That dotes on Cassio, as 'tis the strumpet's plague   95
  To beguile many and be beguiled by one.
  He, when he hears of her, cannot refrain
  From the excess of laughter. Here he comes.

[*Re-enter Cassio.*]

  As he shall smile, Othello shall go mad;
  And his unbookish jealousy must construe   100
  Poor Cassio's smiles, gestures, and light behaviour
  Quite in the wrong. How do you now, lieutenant?
Cassio: The worser that you give me the addition
  Whose want even kills me.
Iago: Ply Desdemona well, and you are sure on't.   105
  Now, if this suit lay in Bianca's power,
  How quickly should you speed!
Cassio: Alas, poor caitiff!
Othello: Look how he laughs already!
Iago: I never knew a woman love man so.
Cassio: Alas, poor rogue! I think, i' faith, she loves me.   110
Othello: Now he denies it faintly, and laughs it out.
Iago: Do you hear, Cassio?
Othello: Now he importunes him
  To tell it o'er. Go to. Well said, well said.
Iago: She gives it out that you shall marry her.
  Do you intend it?   115
Cassio: Ha, ha, ha!
Othello: Do you triumph, Roman? Do you triumph?

118	*customer:* one who purchases sexual services
118–119	*Prithee ... wit:* Please think more kindly of my judgement or intellect. *unwholesome:* unhealthy or corrupted
120	*They ... win:* Literally, "he laughs that wins," or "they who laugh last laugh best."
121	*cry goes:* rumour has it
123	*very:* true; *else:* otherwise
124	*scored me:* settled my account, or, possibly, branded or wounded me
125	*the monkey's ... out:* a term of playful contempt usually applied to children, here to Bianca and what she says
126	*love and flattery:* love of me and flattery of herself
128	*beckons:* signals to
129	*even:* just
131	*bauble:* a plaything; a childish or foolish person
132	*falls me thus:* a demonstration of how Bianca embraced him
133	*imports:* implies or signifies
134	*lolls:* lounges against me; literally, dangles from; *hales:* hauls

139	*Before me:* on my word, a milder version of the oath before God
140	*such another fitchew:* another of the same sort, that is, such a prostitute. A fitchew is a polecat, a longhaired, very smelly member of the weasel family also known for its vigour during mating. Applied to a person, it suggests vileness and loose morals. *perfumed:* Prostitutes used a great deal of perfume.
142	*Let:* may; *dam:* mother (dame)—in proverbs, the devil's mother was more evil than the devil himself
144	*take out:* copy
144–145	*piece of work:* a likely story
147	*hobby-horse:* loose woman, prostitute or possibly a mistress
148	*on't:* from it
150	*should:* must
151	*An:* if
152	*when ... for:* when next I make preparations for you or when I next invite you, which will be never

Cassio: I marry her? What, a customer? Prithee, bear some charity
    to my wit; do not think it so unwholesome. Ha, ha, ha!

Othello: So, so, so, so! They laugh that win.   120

Iago: Faith, the cry goes that you shall marry her.

Cassio: Prithee, say true.

Iago: I am a very villain else.

Othello: Have you scored me? Well.

Cassio: This is the monkey's own giving out. She is persuaded I   125
    will marry her out of her own love and flattery, not out of
    my promise.

Othello: Iago beckons me; now he begins the story.

Cassio: She was here even now; she haunts me in every place. I
    was the other day talking on the sea bank with certain   130
    Venetians, and thither comes the bauble, and, by this hand,
    she falls me thus about my neck—

Othello: Crying "O dear Cassio!" as it were. His gesture imports it.

Cassio: So hangs, and lolls, and weeps upon me; so hales and
    pulls me. Ha, ha, ha!   135

Othello: Now he tells how she plucked him to my chamber. O, I
    see that nose of yours, but not that dog I shall throw it to.

Cassio: Well, I must leave her company.

Iago: Before me! Look where she comes.

Cassio: 'Tis such another fitchew! Marry, a perfumed one.   140

   [*Enter Bianca.*]

   What do you mean by this haunting of me?

Bianca: Let the devil and his dam haunt you! What did you mean
    by that same handkerchief you gave me even now? I was a
    fine fool to take it. I must take out the work? A likely piece
    of work that you should find it in your chamber and know   145
    not who left it there! This is some minx's token, and I must
    take out the work? There! Give it your hobby-horse.
    Wheresoever you had it, I'll take out no work on't.

Cassio: How now, my sweet Bianca? How now? how now?

Othello: By heaven, that should be my handkerchief!   150

Bianca: An you'll come to supper to-night, you may: an you will
    not, come when you are next prepared for.   [*Exit.*]

157   *fain:* gladly

166   *prizes:* regards or esteems (used sarcastically)

173   *I strike it:* obviously suggesting an appropriate gesture

177   *your way:* like you, or the way you should think

180–181 *wit and invention:* intelligence and inventiveness, or perhaps understanding and imagination

185   *gentle:* mild or yielding; a sarcastic response by Iago to Othello's use of the term

188   *fond over:* doting; *patent:* permission or special privilege
189   *touch ... nobody:* If it doesn't bother you, it doesn't bother anybody.

Iago: After her, after her!

Cassio: Faith, I must; she'll rail i' the street else.

Iago: Will you sup there? 155

Cassio: Yes, I intend so.

Iago: Well, I may chance to see you; for I would very fain speak
    with you.

Cassio: Prithee, come. Will you?

Iago: Go to; say no more.   [*Exit Cassio.*] 160

Othello: [*Advancing.*] How shall I murder him, Iago?

Iago: Did you perceive how he laughed at his vice?

Othello: O Iago!

Iago: And did you see the handkerchief?

Othello: Was that mine? 165

Iago: Yours, by this hand. And to see how he prizes the foolish
    woman your wife! She gave it him, and he hath given it his
    whore.

Othello: I would have him nine years a-killing! A fine woman! A
    fair woman! A sweet woman! 170

Iago: Nay, you must forget that.

Othello: Ay, let her rot, and perish, and be damned to-night; for
    she shall not live. No, my heart is turned to stone; I strike it,
    and it hurts my hand. O, the world hath not a sweeter
    creature. She might lie by an emperor's side and command 175
    him tasks.

Iago: Nay, that's not your way.

Othello: Hang her! I do but say what she is. So delicate with
    her needle! An admirable musician! O, she will sing the
    savageness out of a bear! Of so high and plenteous wit 180
    and invention—

Iago: She's the worse for all this.

Othello: O, a thousand thousand times! And then, of so gentle a
    condition!

Iago: Ay, too gentle. 185

Othello: Nay, that's certain; but yet the pity of it, Iago! O Iago, the
    pity of it, Iago!

Iago: If you are so fond over her iniquity, give her patent to offend;
    for, if it touch not you, it comes near nobody.

190   *messes:* servings of meat, as in "chop her into little pieces"

194   *expostulate:* to argue, to set forth grievances
195   *unprovide my mind:* make me unwilling; unsettle or disarm me

197   *even the:* the very

200   *be his undertaker:* he who undertakes to kill him, that is, he
        who does work for another

205   *With all my heart:* I wish it with all my heart, or I thank you
        with all my heart.

207   *the instrument ... pleasures:* the letter (formal document)
        containing their wishes or commands

213   *fall'n:* happened
214   *unkind:* unfortunate

218   *in:* with
219   *'twixt:* between

Othello: I will chop her into messes! Cuckold me!   190

Iago: O, 'tis foul in her.

Othello: With mine officer!

Iago: That's fouler.

Othello: Get me some poison, Iago, this night. I'll not expostulate
    with her, lest her body and beauty unprovide my mind   195
    again. This night, Iago!

Iago: Do it not with poison. Strangle her in her bed, even the bed
    she hath contaminated.

Othello: Good, good! The justice of it pleases. Very good!

Iago: And for Cassio, let me be his undertaker: you shall hear   200
    more by midnight.

Othello: Excellent good. [*A trumpet within.*] What trumpet is that
    same?

Iago: Something from Venice, sure.

    [*Enter Lodovico, Desdemona, and Attendants.*]

                       'Tis Lodovico,
    Come from the Duke; and see, your wife is with him.

Lodovico: God save you, worthy general!

Othello: With all my heart, sir.   205

Lodovico: The Duke and Senators of Venice greet you.
                            [*Gives him a letter.*]

Othello: I kiss the instrument of their pleasures.
                        [*Opens the letter and reads.*]

Desdemona: And what's the news, good cousin Lodovico?

Iago: I am very glad to see you, signior.
    Welcome to Cyprus.   210

Lodovico: I thank you. How does Lieutenant Cassio?

Iago: Lives, sir.

Desdemona: Cousin, there's fall'n between him and my lord
    An unkind breach; but you shall make all well.

Othello: Are you sure of that?   215

Desdemona: My lord?

Othello: [*Reads.*] *This fail you not to do as you will—*

Lodovico: He did not call; he's busy in the paper.
    Is there division 'twixt thy lord and Cassio?

Desdemona: A most unhappy one. I would do much   220

221   *atone:* reconcile

222   *Are you wise:* Are you in your right mind in reference to your remark about your love for Cassio?

225   *Deputing ... government:* appointing Cassio in his place as governor
226   *troth:* faith

227   *mad:* likely foolish, rather than insane

231   *very:* too

233   *teem with:* give birth to or bring forth, as in tears
234   *falls:* lets fall (of crocodile tears); *crocodile:* The crocodile was regarded as the most deceitful of animals, shedding tears to lure people to destruction.

240   *turn:* turn back
241   *turn:* repeatedly change or be fickle and therefore unfaithful

245   *well-painted passion:* well-faked emotion

247   *anon:* soon

To atone them, for the love I bear to Cassio.
Othello: Fire and brimstone!
Desdemona: My lord?
Othello: Are you wise?
Desdemona: What, is he angry?
Lodovico: May be the letter moved him;
  For, as I think, they do command him home,
  Deputing Cassio in his government.   225
Desdemona: By my troth, I am glad on't.
Othello: Indeed?
Desdemona: My lord?
Othello: I am glad to see you mad.
Desdemona: Why, sweet Othello—
Othello: Devil!   [*Striking her.*]
Desdemona: I have not deserved this.
Lodovico: My lord, this would not be believed in Venice,   230
  Though I should swear I saw't. 'Tis very much.
  Make her amends; she weeps.
Othello: O devil, devil!
  If that the earth could teem with woman's tears,
  Each drop she falls would prove a crocodile.
  Out of my sight!
Desdemona: I will not stay to offend you.   [*Going.*]   235
Lodovico: Truly, an obedient lady.
  I do beseech your lordship call her back.
Othello: Mistress!
Desdemona: My lord?
Othello: What would you with her, sir?
Lodovico: Who, I, my lord?
Othello: Ay! You did wish that I would make her turn.   240
  Sir, she can turn, and turn, and yet go on
  And turn again; and she can weep, sir, weep;
  And she's obedient, as you say, obedient,
  Very obedient. Proceed you in your tears.
  Concerning this, sir—O well-painted passion!   245
  I am commanded home. Get you away;
  I'll send for you anon. Sir, I obey the mandate

249	*place:* official position
251	*Goats and monkeys:* (see Act 3, Scene 3, line 403) "as prime as goats, as hot as monkeys," believed to be very sexually active animals
253	*all in all sufficient:* capable or competent in every way
254	*virtue:* moral excellence or manliness
257	*safe:* in good health, that is, is he sane
258	*that:* that which; *censure:* opinion or judgement about
260	*I would:* I wish. Iago is suggesting that he fears Othello may be insane (which could at least provide an explanation for his terrible actions).
262	*use:* habit or custom
263	*blood:* emotions
267	*courses will denote:* conduct or actions will reveal

And will return to Venice. Hence, avaunt!   [*Exit Desdemona.*]
Cassio shall have my place. And, sir, to-night
I do entreat that we may sup together.   250
    You are welcome, sir, to Cyprus. Goats and monkeys!   [*Exit.*]
Lodovico: Is this the noble Moor whom our full Senate
    Call all in all sufficient? Is this the nature
    Whom passion could not shake? Whose solid virtue
    The shot of accident nor dart of chance   255
    Could neither graze nor pierce?
Iago: He is much changed.
Lodovico: Are his wits safe? Is he not light of brain?
Iago: He's that he is; I may not breathe my censure
    What he might be. If what he might he is not,
    I would to heaven he were!
Lodovico: What, strike his wife?   260
Iago: Faith, that was not so well; yet would I knew
    That stroke would prove the worst!
Lodovico: Is it his use?
    Or did the letters work upon his blood
    And new-create this fault?
Iago: Alas, alas!
    It is not honesty in me to speak   265
    What I have seen and known. You shall observe him,
    And his own courses will denote him so
    That I may save my speech. Do but go after
    And mark how he continues.
Lodovico: I am sorry that I am deceived in him.   [*Exeunt.*] 270

Act 4, Scene 1: Activities

1. Lines 1–90 outline a conversation between Othello and Iago in which Iago wreaks havoc on Othello's emotional and mental state. Othello appears totally reckless here and essentially throws away his career by acting exactly the opposite of how a military commander is expected to conduct himself. Of course, Iago orchestrates the whole encounter. As a director, decide how you want these speeches delivered. Does Othello act consistently irrational, angry, out of control, or is he despondent? Does he go through emotional swings? What is his tone of voice? What is Iago's? Write your instructions clearly and carefully so that the actors can produce the effect you want. Rehearse this sequence with members of your group to see how well it works and how effective it is. You could tape your version for the rest of the class to comment on.

2. Storyboarding is a technique used by directors to decide how a scene is to be filmed. It employs a picture-frame format, one frame per shot accompanied by a key line of text for each one. Choose a short exchange from this scene, and storyboard it for a television production of the play. Remember, television, because of its small-screen format, uses many close-up shots to direct the viewer's attention to key elements of the scene. Sketch approximately 10 shots that clearly show how you are going to film this sequence. If you have access to a video camera, you can actually tape the scene after you have rehearsed it with volunteers from your group. Show your version to the class for their reaction.

3. One of the most devastating pieces of "information" Iago gives to Othello is about Desdemona's supposed sexual infidelity. How does Iago accomplish this? Is this another fabrication, or does Iago really believe it? Do you think he is in love with Desdemona? Is this a spur-of-the-moment act, or has Iago planned it all along? Discuss these questions with your group, and come up with an explanation of the encounter that is agreed to by everyone. Remember to take

into account Iago's aside in lines 43–47. Write your own account of it in your journal.

4. Many events happen in this scene that sound as if they came from a TV soap opera. For instance, Othello, on Iago's instructions, hides and overhears what he thinks is Cassio talking about his love for Desdemona; Cassio is really talking about Bianca and knows nothing of the scheme Iago is hatching. Bianca enters and mentions the handkerchief; Cassio leaves, and Othello emerges filled with anger and revenge. However, this is no soap. With a partner, discuss what keeps it from "soap" status. These events all pile up on each other. What effect does that have? You are Othello. Given your present state of mind, what is the effect of all of this on you as you listen? Write an interior monologue for Othello in which you show his thought processes at work.

5. Othello seems obsessed with the idea that he is now a cuckold. This term has fallen out of common use, but it means the husband of an unfaithful wife. The origins of the word are unclear, but some suggest that it refers to the female cuckoo's habit of laying her eggs in the nests of other birds. Cuckolds were always depicted as having antlers or horns, and Othello uses this reference. What is your explanation for this association? In your group, decide whether Othello is more concerned with his damaged ego than he is with the reasons for his wife's supposed infidelity, or whether there might be another reason entirely. What does this suggest to you about male-female relationships in this play? Do you feel that these issues still exist? Write a paper suggesting your solutions to the problem. Draw or make a collage showing your visual image of a cuckold.

6. Othello has already decided to kill his wife with poison. With a partner, discuss why Iago suggests an even more gruesome means of death. What might be going on in Iago's mind at this time? Write an aside for him that might make that clear.

7. One point of view holds that Othello is not stupid: he believes Iago because Iago is his trusted officer. The two

fought together, drank together, dreamt together, and presumably womanized together. Iago was wronged. He should have had the lieutenancy instead of Cassio, who never fought in a war, and who was wealthy and sheltered. Iago has a right to be bitter. He is just out of control, not calculating and mean.

Use this perspective as the basis for a class debate. You may need to review the protocol used in debates before you proceed.

8. The arrival of the contingent from Venice interrupts everything. This is an obvious dramatic device. Discuss what purpose it serves and why it wasn't used earlier (or even later). Write your version of the letter from the Duke. What is Othello's response to it?

9. Desdemona somehow feels the need to inform Lodovico about Cassio's plight. Why does she do this? After reading the letter, Othello strikes Desdemona. Would you include this in your production of the play? If you decide to, how would you direct Desdemona's reaction to it? Do you see her as a passive, witless victim, or is she an example of amazing stoicism? Is she, in fact, as innocent as she appears? What does her reaction to this blow tell us about her? If the act is omitted, what message does that deliver? Present your conclusions to others in the class.

10. Lodovico's final comment is, "I am sorry that I am deceived in him" (meaning Othello). How did all of this come about, and what is important about it? What is Iago's role in drawing forth this conclusion? How many times has Iago used the word "honesty" in this scene? Is he honest in his own mind? If he is, to whom is he honest? Is there possibly another motive behind what Iago says to Lodovico? If you were Lodovico, would you conclude that Othello has lost his mind?

For the next scene ...

Describe a TV or movie character whom you would consider gullible. What do you think makes a person so easily tricked or deceived?

Act 4, Scene 2

In this scene ...

Othello, in discussion with Emilia, refuses to believe her defence of Desdemona, and insinuates that Emilia is the madam of a brothel and Desdemona is one of her prostitutes. When Desdemona enters, Othello accuses her openly of being a whore. She swears her loyalty but Othello is convinced that she has sworn a false oath and maintains his resolve to kill her. He calls Emilia, tosses money at her, and leaves. Desdemona now turns to Iago for help in pleading her case to Othello. He reassures her that Othello is only upset at being recalled to Venice, and he sends her to dine with her guests. Roderigo then enters and accuses Iago of inaction on his behalf, saying he has run out of money and patience. Iago insists that Roderigo can still win Desdemona. He tells Roderigo that Othello is to leave for Mauritania with Desdemona, leaving Cassio to take his place in Cyprus. However, if Roderigo will kill Cassio, then Othello and Desdemona will have to remain in Cyprus, thus allowing Roderigo's hopes to be realized. Once again, Roderigo allows himself to be convinced.

5   *made up:* formed

9   *mask:* Venetian ladies wore masks.

12   *durst:* dare; *honest:* faithful or chaste
13   *Lay ... stake:* wager my life on it; *other:* otherwise
14   *abuse:* deceive or wrong

16   *Let ... curse:* Let God punish him with the same curse he
        used to afflict the serpent in the Garden of Eden.
18   *happy:* fortunate

20   *She:* Emilia
20–21   *yet she's ... much:* The most artless brothel-keeper can tell
        the same sort of story. *bawd:* woman who runs a brothel
22   *closet lock and key:* a private room or chest with lock and
        key

Scene 2

A room in the castle.
Enter Othello and Emilia.

Othello: You have seen nothing then?

Emilia: Nor ever heard, nor ever did suspect.

Othello: Yes, you have seen Cassio and she together.

Emilia: But then I saw no harm, and then I heard

    Each syllable that breath made up between them.   5

Othello: What, did they never whisper?

Emilia: Never, my lord.

Othello: Nor send you out o' the way?

Emilia: Never.

Othello: To fetch her fan, her gloves, her mask, nor nothing?

Emilia: Never, my lord.   10

Othello: That's strange.

Emilia: I durst, my lord, to wager she is honest,

    Lay down my soul at stake. If you think other,

    Remove your thought; it doth abuse your bosom.

    If any wretch have put this in your head,   15

    Let heaven requite it with the serpent's curse!

    For if she be not honest, chaste, and true,

    There's no man happy; the purest of their wives

    Is foul as slander.

Othello: Bid her come hither. Go.   *[Exit Emilia.]*

    She says enough; yet she's a simple bawd   20

    That cannot say as much. This is a subtle whore,

    A closet lock and key of villainous secrets;

    And yet she'll kneel and pray; I have seen her do't.

    [Enter Desdemona and Emilia.]

Desdemona: My lord, what is your will?

27–28   *Some ... door:* Othello is treating Emilia as if she is a
brothel-keeper, with certain duties to perform, and Desdemona
is one of the inmates under her charge. *procreants:* those who
copulate or procreate; that is, the prostitute and her customer

30   *mystery:* trade (as a bawd); *dispatch:* hurry

36   *Lest:* for fear that; *being ... heaven:* because you are as
beautiful as an angel

36–37   These lines suggest that devils only transport to hell those
who truly belong to them in spirit.

42   *heavy:* sorrowful
43   *motive:* cause
44   *haply:* by chance or perhaps
45   *An instrument:* to be the cause of; *calling back:* being
recalled to Venice

48   *try:* test

54–55   *A fixed ... finger at:* the fixed (frozen) target of scorn and
derision at whom time points its slowly and inexorably moving finger. "Time of scorn" describes time itself, which
moves as imperceptibly as the hand on a clock. The image
is a complicated one.

Othello: Pray, chuck, come hither.
Desdemona: What is your pleasure?
Othello: Let me see your eyes.   25
    Look in my face.
Desdemona: What horrible fancy's this?
Othello: [*To Emilia.*] Some of your function, mistress.
    Leave procreants alone and shut the door;
    Cough or cry hem if anybody come.
    Your mystery, your mystery. Nay, dispatch!   [*Exit Emilia.*]   30
Desdemona: Upon my knees, what doth your speech import?
    I understand a fury in your words,
    But not the words.
Othello: Why, what art thou?
Desdemona: Your wife, my lord; your true
    And loyal wife.
Othello: Come, swear it, damn thyself;   35
    Lest, being like one of heaven, the devils themselves
    Should fear to seize thee. Therefore be doubledamn'd.
    Swear thou art honest.
Desdemona: Heaven doth truly know it.
Othello: Heaven truly knows that thou art false as hell.
Desdemona: To whom, my lord? With whom? How am I false?   40
Othello: Ah, Desdemon! Away! Away! Away!
Desdemona: Alas the heavy day! Why do you weep?
    Am I the motive of these tears, my lord?
    If haply you my father do suspect
    An instrument of this your calling back,   45
    Lay not your blame on me. If you have lost him,
    Why, I have lost him too.
Othello: Had it pleased heaven
    To try me with affliction, had they rain'd
    All kinds of sores and shames on my bare head,
    Steep'd me in poverty to the very lips,   50
    Given to captivity me and my utmost hopes,
    I should have found in some place of my soul
    A drop of patience. But, alas, to make me
    A fixed figure for the time of scorn

57	*there:* in his love for Desdemona; *garner'd up:* stored or treasured
59	*fountain:* spring or source
61	*cistern:* a reservoir for storing water, but frequently a stagnant pool of standing water, or a cesspool
62	*knot and gender:* couple and mate, that is, copulate
62–64	*Turn ... hell:* another complex image. Possibly, even (smiling) Patience (depicted as rose-lipped) will turn pale and grim at this spectacle. *cherubin:* traditionally depicted as rosy-cheeked, smiling baby angels
66–67	*as summer ... blowing:* A "shambles" is a slaughterhouse. "Quicken" means to be filled with life or become pregnant (and deposit their eggs).
70	*ignorant:* unknown, unintentional
71	*fair paper:* a reference to Desdemona
73	*commoner:* a common whore
74	*I should ... cheeks:* roughly, "my cheeks would burn." A forge is a blacksmith's furnace used to heat metal.
77	*it:* that which you have committed; *moon winks:* The moon shuts her eyes. The moon has a long association with Diana, the goddess of chastity.
79	*mine of earth:* an underground cave where, in mythology, the winds were believed to reside
83	*vessel:* body

To point his slow unmoving finger at!   55
Yet could I bear that too; well, very well.
But there where I have garner'd up my heart,
Where either I must live or bear no life,
The fountain from the which my current runs
Or else dries up; to be discarded thence,   60
Or keep it as a cistern for foul toads
To knot and gender in! Turn thy complexion there,
Patience, thou young and rose-lipp'd cherubin—
Ay, there look grim as hell!
Desdemona: I hope my noble lord esteems me honest.   65
Othello: O, ay; as summer flies are in the shambles,
   That quicken even with blowing. O thou weed,
   Who art so lovely fair, and smell'st so sweet
   That the sense aches at thee, would thou hadst ne'er been born!
Desdemona: Alas, what ignorant sin have I committed?   70
Othello: Was this fair paper, this most goodly book,
   Made to write "whore" upon? What committed?
   Committed? O thou public commoner!
   I should make very forges of my cheeks
   That would to cinders burn up modesty,   75
   Did I but speak thy deeds. What committed?
   Heaven stops the nose at it, and the moon winks;
   The bawdy wind, that kisses all it meets,
   Is hush'd within the hollow mine of earth
   And will not hear it. What committed?   80
   Impudent strumpet!
Desdemona: By heaven, you do me wrong!
Othello: Are not you a strumpet?
Desdemona: No, as I am a Christian.
   If to preserve this vessel for my lord
   From any other foul unlawful touch
   Be not to be a strumpet, I am none.   85
Othello: What, not a whore?
Desdemona: No, as I shall be saved!
Othello: Is't possible?
Desdemona: O, heaven forgive us!

88	*I cry you mercy:* I mistook you for (therefore, I beg your pardon)
90	*You, mistress:* Emilia
91	*Saint Peter:* the keeper of the gate of heaven
92	*keep ... hell:* The biblical reference indicates the keys of heaven shall unlock the gates of hell; here, the way to hell is through the harlot's house.
93	*done our course:* completed our business
94	*counsel:* secret; that is, reveal nothing
95	*conceive:* imagine or think
104	*go by water:* be expressed with tears
107	*meet:* proper
108–109	*stick ... misuse:* fasten the slightest suspicion to my smallest fault
115	*bewhored:* talked to her as if she were a whore
116	*despite:* anger and abuse; *heavy terms:* angry and distressing words

Othello: I cry you mercy then.
  I took you for that cunning whore of Venice
  That married with Othello. [*Raising his voice.*] You, mistress,   90
  That have the office opposite to Saint Peter
  And keep the gate of hell!

[*Re-enter Emilia.*]

                           You, you, ay, you!
  We have done our course; there's money for your pains:
  I pray you, turn the key, and keep our counsel.   [*Exit.*]
Emilia: Alas, what does this gentleman conceive?   95
  How do you, madam? How do you, my good lady?
Desdemona: Faith, half asleep.
Emilia: Good madam, what's the matter with my lord?
Desdemona: With who?
Emilia: Why, with my lord, madam.   100
Desdemona: Who is thy lord?
Emilia: He that is yours, sweet lady.
Desdemona: I have none. Do not talk to me, Emilia.
  I cannot weep; nor answer have I none
  But what should go by water. Prithee, to-night
  Lay on my bed my wedding sheets. Remember;   105
  And call thy husband hither.
Emilia: Here's a change indeed!   [*Exit.*]
Desdemona: 'Tis meet I should be used so, very meet.
  How have I been behaved, that he might stick
  The small'st opinion on my least misuse?

[*Re-enter Emilia, with Iago.*]

Iago: What is your pleasure, madam? How is't with you?   110
Desdemona: I cannot tell. Those that do teach young babes
  Do it with gentle means and easy tasks:
  He might have chid me so; for, in good faith,
  I am a child to chiding.
Iago: What is the matter, lady?
Emilia: Alas, Iago, my lord hath so bewhored her,   115
  Thrown such despite and heavy terms upon her
  As true hearts cannot bear.

120	*in his drink:* while drunk
121	*callet:* a slut. This is a term of abuse for women believed to be having sex outside marriage, although it also applies to women who charge money for sex (prostitutes).
128	*Beshrew:* that is, curse him
129	*trick:* strange behaviour
130	*I will be hang'd if:* let me be hanged, that is, I'll bet my life
131	*busy:* meddlesome
132	*cogging:* deceiving; *cozening:* cheating
136	*halter:* hangman's noose
138	*what form:* in what way; *what likelihood:* what proof is there
139	*abused:* deceived
140	*scurvy:* disgusting or contemptible
141	*that:* I hope that; *companions:* people (who are held in contempt, here); *unfold:* will reveal or bring to light
144	*Speak within door:* Speak more softly so no one can hear you outside the door.
145	*squire:* fine fellow (said with contempt)
146	*turn'd ... without:* changed your perception as if it were a garment turned inside out to reveal the seams; made into something ugly

Desdemona: Am I that name, Iago?

Iago: What name, fair lady?

Desdemona: Such as she says my lord did say I was.

Emilia: He called her whore. A beggar in his drink   120
Could not have laid such terms upon his callet.

Iago: Why did he so?

Desdemona: I do not know; I am sure I am none such.

Iago: Do not weep, do not weep. Alas the day!

Emilia: Hath she forsook so many noble matches,   125
Her father and her country, all her friends,
To be call'd whore? Would it not make one weep?

Desdemona: It is my wretched fortune.

Iago: Beshrew him for't!
How comes this trick upon him?

Desdemona: Nay, heaven doth know.

Emilia: I will be hang'd if some eternal villain,   130
Some busy and insinuating rogue,
Some cogging, cozening slave, to get some office,
Have not devised this slander. I'll be hang'd else.

Iago: Fie, there is no such man; it is impossible.

Desdemona: If any such there be, heaven pardon him!   135

Emilia: A halter pardon him! And hell gnaw his bones!
Why should he call her whore? Who keeps her company?
What place? what time? what form? what likelihood?
The Moor's abused by some most villainous knave,
Some base notorious knave, some scurvy fellow.   140
O heaven, that such companions thou'ldst unfold,
And put in every honest hand a whip
To lash the rascals naked through the world
Even from the east to the west!

Iago: Speak within door.

Emilia: O, fie upon them! Some such squire he was   145
That turn'd your wit the seamy side without
And made you to suspect me with the Moor.

Iago: You are a fool. Go to.

Desdemona: O good Iago,
What shall I do to win my lord again?

153	*discourse of thought:* the course of my thinking
154	*that:* if

156	*yet:* still

159	*Comfort forswear me:* May relief (in distress) abandon me.
160	*defeat:* ruin or destroy

163	*addition:* title
164	*world's ... vanity:* all the world's wealth or valuable things

166	*does him offence:* causes him pain

170	*stay the meat:* are waiting for supper

175	*daffest ... device:* put me off, distract me with some trick

177	*conveniency:* opportunity; *than:* that
178	*of hope:* for amplifying or increasing my hopes
179	*put up:* put up with

Good friend, go to him; for, by this light of heaven, 150
I know not how I lost him. Here I kneel:
If e'er my will did trespass 'gainst his love
Either in discourse of thought or actual deed,
Or that mine eyes, mine ears, or any sense
Delighted them in any other form, 155
Or that I do not yet, and ever did,
And ever will, though he do shake me off
To beggarly divorcement, love him dearly,
Comfort forswear me! Unkindness may do much;
And his unkindness may defeat my life, 160
But never taint my love. I cannot say "whore."
It doth abhor me now I speak the word;
To do the act that might the addition earn
Not the world's mass of vanity could make me.

Iago: I pray you be content. 'Tis but his humour. 165
The business of the state does him offence,
And he does chide with you.

Desdemona: If 'twere no other—

Iago: 'Tis but so, I warrant.
                                        [*Trumpets within.*]
Hark how these instruments summon you to supper.
The messengers of Venice stay the meat: 170
Go in, and weep not. All things shall be well.
                    [*Exeunt Desdemona and Emilia.*]

[*Enter Roderigo.*]

How now, Roderigo?

Roderigo: I do not find that thou dealest justly with me.

Iago: What in the contrary?

Roderigo: Every day thou daffest me with some device, Iago, 175
    and rather, as it seems to me now, keepest from me all
    conveniency than suppliest me with the least advantage
    of hope. I will indeed no longer endure it; nor am I yet
    persuaded to put up in peace what already I have
    foolishly suffered. 180

Iago: Will you hear me, Roderigo?

183	*are ... together:* do not fit together
185	*naught:* nothing
187	*votarist:* nun
189	*comforts:* encouragement; *sudden respect:* immediate notice
194	*fopped:* deceived
199	*satisfaction:* repayment, in the sense of restoring one's honour by means of a duel
200	*have said:* you have spoken your mind
201–202	*intendment of doing:* is my intention to do
206	*exception:* grievance or fault
207	*directly:* honestly
215	*engines for:* instruments of torture against
216	*within ... compass:* reasonably possible, within the bounds of possibility
217	*depute:* appoint

Roderigo: Faith, I have heard too much; for your words and
    performance are no kin together.

Iago: You charge me most unjustly.

Roderigo: With naught but truth. I have wasted myself out of   185
    means. The jewels you have had from me to deliver
    to Desdemona would half have corrupted a votarist.
    You have told me she hath received them, and returned
    me expectations and comforts of sudden respect and
    acquaintance; but I find none.   190

Iago: Well, go to; very well.

Roderigo: Very well! go to! I cannot go to, man; nor 'tis not very
    well. By this hand, I say 'tis very scurvy, and begin to find
    myself fopped in it.

Iago: Very well.   195

Roderigo: I tell you 'tis not very well. I will make myself known to
    Desdemona. If she will return me my jewels, I will give over
    my suit and repent my unlawful solicitation; if not, assure
    yourself I will seek satisfaction of you.

Iago: You have said now.   200

Roderigo: Ay, and said nothing but what I protest intendment of
    doing.

Iago: Why, now I see there's mettle in thee; and even from this
    instant do build on thee a better opinion than ever before.
    Give me thy hand, Roderigo. Thou hast taken against me   205
    a most just exception; but yet, I protest, I have dealt most
    directly in thy affair.

Roderigo: It hath not appeared.

Iago: I grant indeed it hath not appeared, and your suspicion is
    not without wit and judgement. But, Roderigo, if thou hast   210
    that in thee indeed which I have greater reason to believe
    now than ever, I mean purpose, courage, and valour, this
    night show it. If thou the next night following enjoy not
    Desdemona, take me from this world with treachery and
    devise engines for my life.   215

Roderigo: Well, what is it? Is it within reason and compass?

Iago: Sir, there is especial commission come from Venice to depute
    Cassio in Othello's place.

221   *Mauritania:* the homeland of the North African Moors (later to become Morocco and western Algiers)

222   *abode ... lingered:* his stay is prolonged (extended)

223   *wherein ... determinate:* and no accident can be so decisive in extending his stay

225   *How:* what

226   *uncapable of:* incapable of taking

229   *profit:* benefit

230   *harlotry:* a harlot

232   *fashion to fall out:* arrange to have happen

235   *amazed:* astonished

238   *grows to waste:* nears its end, that is, we are wasting our time discussing all of this

239   *further reason:* additional arguments

Roderigo: Is that true? Why, then Othello and Desdemona return
    again to Venice.   220

Iago: O, no; he goes into Mauritania and takes away with him
    the fair Desdemona, unless his abode be lingered here by
    some accident; wherein none can be so determinate as the
    removing of Cassio.

Roderigo: How do you mean removing of him?   225

Iago: Why, by making him uncapable of Othello's place—knocking
    out his brains.

Roderigo: And that you would have me to do?

Iago: Ay, if you dare do yourself a profit and a right. He sups
    tonight with a harlotry, and thither will I go to him. He   230
    knows not yet of his honourable fortune. If you will watch
    his going thence, which I will fashion to fall out between
    twelve and one, you may take him at your pleasure. I will
    be near to second your attempt, and he shall fall between
    us. Come, stand not amazed at it, but go along with me.   235
    I will show you such a necessity in his death that you shall
    think yourself bound to put it on him. It is now high
    supper-time, and the night grows to waste. About it.

Roderigo: I will hear further reason for this.

Iago: And you shall be satisfied.   [*Exeunt.*] 240

Act 4, Scene 2: Activities

1. When the scene begins, it appears that Emilia and Othello are in the middle of a conversation. Create the conversation as it began up to the point of their entrance. Who do you think approached whom? For what purpose?

2. We are told simply that the setting is "A room in the castle." As a set designer, what specific details would you incorporate in creating the set? You may have to read a significant portion of the scene before you make a decision.

3. In lines 25–90, Othello violently confronts a totally confused Desdemona, who has no idea what has so upset him. Othello's speeches sound like the disconnected ramblings of a madman. Figure out what he is talking about by linking the images he uses with the past events to which they are connected. What does this reveal about what is consuming Othello? Why is he speaking in such a chaotic tumble of language? Write a journal account of Othello's state of mind at this point in the play.

4. At the beginning of the play, Othello appears to be in complete control of himself and of the military forces he is leading. He seems to be governing the island conscientiously and well. With your group, decide what has brought him to the state that we witness in this scene. Is it all Iago's fault? Is anyone else to blame? Has he contributed to it himself? After your discussion, write your own analysis of what you think happened. You might want to use this later as a newspaper account.

5. One of the most wrenching and ironic scenes occurs when Desdemona implores Emilia to ask Iago to intercede with Othello for her. Look up the term "dramatic irony," determine its uses in a play, and indicate the features that lines 110–171 illustrate. How do you think an audience would respond to these exchanges? As a director, what effect would you want to achieve? Indicate this in the notes you prepare for the actors in your production of this portion of the scene.

6. With a partner, discuss how Iago treats Desdemona in their conversation. Is he listening to her? Is he taunting her? Is he wallowing in his own success? Is he frightened by what he has done? Is he impassive? Decide how he might act in this encounter. Iago blames Othello's behaviour on "the business of the state" and assures Desdemona that "all things shall be well." Do you think Desdemona believes this? Why or why not? What do you think Iago means by this last comment? If you have been keeping a profile of Iago, you will want to add your observations about him in this scene to your account.

7. Suddenly, Roderigo reappears in the play. Summarize what goes on between him and Iago. Write an account of what you think has been going on in Roderigo's life up to this point. How is he feeling at this moment? Is he as dull-witted as he appears to be? Is this conversation essential to the play? If you think so, what purpose does it have? If you don't, why would you eliminate it?

For the next scene ...

There is much discussion about marriage and what its obligations are. What are your views on this subject? Should marriage "be forever"?

Act 4, Scene 3

In this scene ...

The company is returning from supper. Intending to
walk with Lodovico, Othello orders Desdemona to go to
bed and to dismiss Emilia. As Emilia assists
Desdemona in preparing for bed, Desdemona reveals
the uneasiness that has plagued her all evening, and
they discuss women who betray their husbands. Emilia
assures Desdemona that many such women exist
because women have the same desires as men do.
Emilia says she would do the same thing if the stakes
were high enough, and argues that women only learn to
behave deceitfully because they are following the
examples set by their deceiving husbands.

7   *be returned:* return

11   *incontinent:* immediately

18   *so would not I:* That's not what I wish. *approve:* praise
19   *stubbornness:* roughness; *checks:* reprimands
20   *have ... them:* attract me by their charm

22   *All's one:* Everything is all right.

Scene 3

Another room in the castle.
Enter Othello, Lodovico, Desdemona,
Emilia, and Attendants.

Lodovico: I do beseech you, sir, trouble yourself no further.

Othello: O, pardon me; 'twill do me good to walk.

Lodovico: Madam, good night. I humbly thank your ladyship.

Desdemona: Your honour is most welcome.

Othello: Will you walk, sir?

O, Desdemona—   5

Desdemona: My lord?

Othello: Get you to bed on the instant; I will be returned forthwith.

    Dismiss your attendant there. Look't be done.

Desdemona: I will, my lord.

                [Exeunt Othello, Lodovico, and Attendants.]

Emilia: How goes it now? He looks gentler than he did.   10

Desdemona: He says he will return incontinent.

    He hath commanded me to go to bed,

    And bade me to dismiss you.

Emilia: Dismiss me?

Desdemona: It was his bidding; therefore, good Emilia,

    Give me my nightly wearing, and adieu.   15

    We must not now displease him.

Emilia: I would you had never seen him!

Desdemona: So would not I. My love doth so approve him

    That even his stubbornness, his checks, his frowns—

    Prithee unpin me—have grace and favour in them.   20

Emilia: I have laid those sheets you bade me on the bed.

Desdemona: All's one. Good faith, how foolish are our minds!

    If I do die before thee, prithee, shroud me

    In one of those same sheets.

Emilia: Come, come, you talk.

27   *Willow:* the symbol of sorrow or grief for lost love or the loss of a loved one

28   *fortune:* what happened to her

30–31   *I have ... side:* It is all I can do to keep from hanging myself, or, perhaps, letting my head fall down in despair.

32   *sing ... Barbara:* The song is from a ballad called "A Lover's Complaint," about a man being forsaken of his love, from *Percy's Reliques.* In that piece, it is the lament of a man; in this play it is the lament of a woman.

34   *proper:* appealing

37   *would:* who would

38   *nether:* lower

46   *Lay by these:* Ignore these things (perhaps the things that she is singing).

48   *hie thee:* go quickly; *anon:* soon or immediately

50   *approve:* agree with

55   *moe:* more

57   *bode:* predict, as in forbode

Desdemona: My mother had a maid call'd Barbara.   25
    She was in love; and he she loved proved mad
    And did forsake her. She had a song of "Willow";
    An old thing 'twas; but it express'd her fortune,
    And she died singing it. That song to-night
    Will not go from my mind; I have much to do   30
    But to go hang my head all at one side
    And sing it like poor Barbara. Prithee, dispatch.
Emilia: Shall I go fetch your night-gown?
Desdemona: No, unpin me here.
    This Lodovico is a proper man.
Emilia: A very handsome man.   35
Desdemona: He speaks well.
Emilia: I know a lady in Venice would have walked
    barefoot to Palestine for a touch of his nether lip.
Desdemona: [*Singing.*]
    The poor soul sat sighing by a sycamore tree,
      Sing all a green willow;   40
    Her hand on her bosom, her head on her knee,
      Sing willow, willow, willow.
    The fresh streams ran by her and murmur'd her moans;
      Sing willow, willow, willow;
    Her salt tears fell from her, and soften'd the stones—   45
    Lay by these. [*Singing.*]
      Sing willow, willow, willow—
    Prithee hie thee; he'll come anon. [*Singing.*]
    Sing all a green willow must be my garland.
    Let nobody blame him; his scorn I approve—   50
    Nay, that's not next. Hark! Who is't that knocks?
Emilia: It's the wind.
Desdemona: [*Singing.*]
    I call'd my love false love; but what said he then?
      Sing willow, willow, willow;
    If I court moe women, you'll couch with moe men.   55
    So, get thee gone; good night. Mine eyes do itch.
    Doth that bode weeping?
Emilia: 'Tis neither here nor there.

60 *abuse:* deceive or ill-use

61 *In ... kind:* in such an obscene way or in such a disgusting manner

63 *by ... light:* an oath probably meaning "by the light of heaven"

67 *price:* prize; *vice:* indiscretion

70 *Marry:* indeed; *joint-ring:* a ring made of two distinct halves that fit together to make one ring—presumably a symbol of the union of husband and wife

71 *measures of lawn:* lawn is linen, so lengths of linen cloth

72 *petty exhibition:* trivial gifts

77 *having:* possessing

78 *for:* in exchange for

79 *might:* could

81 *to the vantage:* besides; *vantage:* something added for good measure; *store:* fill or populate as in "fill up with"

82 *played for:* gambled for. "Played" means wagered, possibly a pun meaning engaged in sexual sport.

84 *they:* husbands; *slack:* neglect; *duties:* to their wives; sexual duties

86 *peevish:* childish, silly or spiteful

87 *Throwing:* imposing

88 *scant ... despite:* reduce our allowance out of spite or malice

89 *galls:* things we resent or feel bitter about; *grace:* forgiveness or mercy

91 *They:* wives

Desdemona: I have heard it said so. O, these men, these men!
   Dost thou in conscience think—tell me, Emilia—
   That there be women do abuse their husbands   60
   In such gross kind?
Emilia: There be some such, no question.
Desdemona: Wouldst thou do such a deed for all the world?
Emilia: Why, would not you?
Desdemona: No, by this heavenly light!
Emilia: Nor I neither by this heavenly light. I might do't as well
   i' the dark.   65
Desdemona: Wouldst thou do such a deed for all the world?
Emilia: The world's a huge thing; it is a great price for a small vice.
Desdemona: In troth, I think thou wouldst not.
Emilia: In troth, I think I should; and undo't when I had done it.
   Marry, I would not do such a thing for a joint-ring, nor for   70
   measures of lawn, nor for gowns, petticoats, nor caps, nor
   any petty exhibition; but for all the whole world—why,
   who would not make her husband a cuckold to make him
   a monarch? I should venture purgatory for't.
Desdemona: Beshrew me if I would do such a wrong for the   75
   whole world.
Emilia: Why, the wrong is but a wrong i' the world; and having
   the world for your labour, 'tis a wrong in your own world,
   and you might quickly make it right.
Desdemona: I do not think there is any such woman.   80
Emilia: Yes, a dozen; and as many to the vantage as would store
   the world they played for.
   But I do think it is their husbands' faults
   If wives do fall. Say that they slack their duties
   And pour our treasures into foreign laps;   85
   Or else break out in peevish jealousies,
   Throwing restraint upon us; or say they strike us,
   Or scant our former having in despite—
   Why, we have galls; and though we have some grace;
   Yet have we some revenge. Let husbands know   90
   Their wives have sense like them. They see, and smell,
   And have their palates both for sweet and sour,

93	*they:* husbands
94	*change:* exchange; *sport:* sexual play
95	*affection:* lust
96	*frailty:* weakness

| 99 | *use:* treat; *else:* or else |

| 101 | *Heaven ... uses send:* Heaven use me or treat me well |
| 102 | *Not ... mend:* not to differentiate what is bad from bad, but to improve by knowledge of what is bad. Or, perhaps, may God show me how to avoid the lessons of wrongdoers and show me how to better myself by not following their example. |

As husbands have. What is it that they do
When they change us for others? Is it sport?
I think it is. And doth affection breed it?   95
I think it doth. Is't frailty that thus errs?
It is so too. And have not we affections,
Desires for sport, and frailty, as men have?
Then let them use us well; else let them know,
The ills we do, their ills instruct us so.   100
Desdemona: Good night, good night. Heaven me such uses send,
Not to pick bad from bad, but by bad mend!   [*Exeunt.*]

Act 4, Scene 3: Activities

1. In this scene, Emilia somewhat cynically philosophizes about how men contribute to the "fall" of wives. Summarize Emilia's argument and determine why she might come to such conclusions. What comments would you add?

2. As the scene ends, Emilia comments about men, "the ills we do, their ills instruct us so." Write a soliloquy for Emilia as an extension of this scene in which she looks back and thinks about what she has observed happening during the course of the play so far. You might want to consider how she views her relationship with Desdemona, how she views Desdemona as a person, and how Desdemona has reacted to Othello's treatment of her. With what kind of expression would you want this soliloquy to be delivered?

3. In this scene, Emilia prepares Desdemona for bed for what turns out to be the last time. The scene is full of haunting and ominous images of death, culminating in Desdemona's song, a gloomy old ballad about betrayal. Why would Desdemona recall this particular ballad? What do you think are the key images in it? What is its effect on you? How do you think an audience would react to the song and the scene itself? Select a piece of music that you feel would be appropriate for her song, and explain your choice.

4. In the eighteenth and nineteenth centuries, productions of *Othello* routinely cut this scene. Why do you suppose this was done? Is it justifiable to do so, in your view? Some productions cut only the "Willow Song." What effect would that have on the scene? Can you make a solid argument for keeping the entire scene intact? After discussion with your group, write your thoughts about these questions in an essay entitled "Interpretations of Othello, Act 4, Scene 3."

Act 4: Consider the Whole Act

1. As Iago, in this act, you seem to have complete control over everything that is happening in the play. Explain, in your diary entry, why you believe that further action is necessary.

2. In this act, Othello seems to undergo a complete shift in character. With your group, discuss how and why this happens.

3. "Wisdom," or "wit and judgement" are terms used throughout this act. Images used in connection with characters help an audience define them. With your group, make a list of the images associated with Othello, Iago, Desdemona, and Emilia. How do these images work to reinforce character portrayal?

4. One observer noted that Act 4 is "a drive toward madness." In your journal, discuss how would you assess this observation. You may wish to share your insights with the class.

5. Despite what has occurred in this act, Desdemona decrees, "Let nobody blame him; his scorn I approve." What would lead her to such a conclusion after all that has just happened to her? Given the opportunity, what advice would you offer her? Record your thoughts as part of the advice column you write for a national newspaper.

For the next scene ...

Is it possible that a young, well-educated, well-adjusted person could commit unspeakable violent acts? Can you recall a case where this might have happened? How do you explain such a thing?

Act 5, Scene 1

In this scene ...

In the dark street, Roderigo hides behind a building with Iago concealed nearby. When Cassio enters, Roderigo attacks him but misses, and he is then wounded by Cassio. Iago, from behind, wounds Cassio in the leg. Othello hears Cassio cry out and thinks that Iago has killed him according to plan, so he ignores Cassio's pleas and returns to the castle to murder Desdemona. Lodovico and Gratiano enter and hear Roderigo and Cassio crying out, but they fear a possible ambush, so they decide to wait for more help. Iago re-enters, and Cassio begs him for help. When Roderigo also cries out, Iago fatally stabs him. Iago calls for more help, and when the two visitors from Venice come to assist him, he tells them that Cassio was the victim of a planned attack. Bianca enters, and Iago accuses her of being "a party in this injury." Iago is careful to ensure that Lodovico and Gratiano are both convinced of Bianca's involvement. When Emilia enters and hears about the events, she also accuses Bianca. Iago sends Emilia to tell Othello and Desdemona what has just occurred.

1 *bulk:* a structure projecting from the front of a shop, possibly a stall on which goods were displayed for sale; *straight:* right away or immediately

2 *bare:* ready for use; that is, drawn; *put:* drive or plunge; *home:* as far as it will go

6 *miscarry:* fail

11 *quat:* pimple—a term of contempt used for adolescents. Perhaps Roderigo is younger than we at first thought. *to the sense:* to the quick (the most vital or sensitive part of the body)

14 *Live Roderigo:* if Roderigo lives

16 *bobb'd:* deceived, cheated, or swindled

21 *unfold me:* expose me (and my lies)

25 *But:* except; *my coat is better:* a suggestion that he wears an armour undercoat, or perhaps just a suggestion of his toughness

26 *make proof of:* test

Act 5, Scene 1

Cyprus. A street.
Enter Iago and Roderigo.

Iago: Here, stand behind this bulk; straight will he come.
   Wear thy good rapier bare, and put it home.
   Quick, quick! Fear nothing; I'll be at thy elbow.
   It makes us, or it mars us; think on that,
   And fix most firm thy resolution.   5
Roderigo: Be near at hand; I may miscarry in't.
Iago: Here, at thy hand. Be bold, and take thy stand.   *[Retires.]*
Roderigo: I have no great devotion to the deed,
   And yet he hath given me satisfying reasons.
   'Tis but a man gone. Forth my sword! He dies!   10
Iago: I have rubb'd this young quat almost to the sense,
   And he grows angry. Now whether he kill Cassio,
   Or Cassio him, or each do kill the other,
   Every way makes my gain. Live Roderigo,
   He calls me to a restitution large   15
   Of gold and jewels that I bobb'd from him
   As gifts to Desdemona.
   It must not be. If Cassio do remain,
   He hath a daily beauty in his life
   That makes me ugly; and besides, the Moor   20
   May unfold me to him; there stand I in much peril.
   No, he must die. Be't so! I hear him coming.

   [Enter Cassio.]

Roderigo: I know his gait. 'Tis he. Villain, thou diest!
                       [Makes a pass at Cassio.]
Cassio: That thrust had been mine enemy indeed
   But that my coat is better than thou know'st.   25
   I will make proof of thine.

29   *even:* just

31   *he:* Cassio; *brave:* worthy or courageous

33   *Minion:* usually means favourite servant or "darling," but
        applied to Desdemona it likely means "worthless woman"
34   *unblest fate:* meaning she is damned; *hies:* hurries forward
        or hastens nearer
35   *Forth of:* out of or out from

37   *watch:* watchman; *passage:* people passing
38   *'Tis some mischance:* There is something terribly wrong.
        direful: dreadful

42   *heavy:* gloomy and overcast
43   *counterfeits:* tricks, fakes
44   *in to:* (come) near, as in approach

47   *one:* a person who; *in his shirt:* possibly in his night attire or
        without his outer garments
48   *cries on:* shouts or cries out

[Draws, and wounds Roderigo.]

Roderigo: O, I am slain!

[Iago from behind wounds Cassio in the leg, and exit.]

Cassio: I am maim'd for ever. Help, ho! Murder! Murder! *[Falls.]*

   [Enter Othello.]

Othello: The voice of Cassio. Iago keeps his word.

Roderigo: O, villain that I am!

Othello: It is even so.

Cassio: O, help, ho! light! a surgeon!   30

Othello: 'Tis he. O brave Iago, honest and just,

   That hast such noble sense of thy friend's wrong!

   Thou teachest me. Minion, your dear lies dead,

   And your unblest fate hies. Strumpet, I come.

   Forth of my heart those charms, thine eyes, are blotted.   35

   Thy bed, lust-stain'd, shall with lust's blood be spotted.

                                        [Exit.]

   [Enter Lodovico and Gratiano.]

Cassio: What, ho? No watch? No passage? Murder! Murder!

Gratiano: 'Tis some mischance. The cry is very direful.

Cassio: O, help!

Lodovico: Hark!   40

Roderigo: O wretched villain!

Lodovico: Two or three groan. It is a heavy night.

   These may be counterfeits. Let's think't unsafe

   To come in to the cry without more help.

Roderigo: Nobody come? Then shall I bleed to death.   45

Lodovico: Hark!

   [Re-enter Iago, with a light.]

Gratiano: Here's one comes in his shirt, with light and weapons.

Iago: Who's there? Whose noise is this that cries on murder?

Lodovico: We do not know.

Iago: Did not you hear a cry?

Cassio: Here, here! For heaven's sake, help me!

Iago: What's the matter?   50

Gratiano: This is Othello's ancient, as I take it.

Lodovico: The same indeed, a very valiant fellow.

255

53   *What:* who
54   *spoil'd, undone:* badly injured or perhaps destroyed

58   *make:* get, as in escape

66   *prove us:* find us to be; *praise:* value or appraise

69   *I cry you mercy:* I beg your pardon

74   *Who is't that cried:* Iago repeats Bianca's question, possibly sarcastically, with the intent to implicate her in the attack.

78   *notable:* known or obvious
78–79 *may ... should be:* do you know who they are

82   *chair:* as in sedan chair; a chair, sometimes enclosed, carried by two bearers; here to act as a litter to carry Cassio

Iago: What are you here that cry so grievously?

Cassio: Iago? O, I am spoil'd, undone by villains!
Give me some help.   55

Iago: O me, lieutenant! What villains have done this?

Cassio: I think that one of them is hereabout
And cannot make away.

Iago: O treacherous villains!
[*To Lodovico and Gratiano.*] What are you there? Come in,
and give some help.

Roderigo: O, help me here!   60

Cassio: That's one of them.

Iago: O murderous slave! O villain!
[*Stabs Roderigo.*]

Roderigo: O damn'd Iago! O inhuman dog!

Iago: Kill men i' the dark?—Where be these bloody thieves?
How silent is this town! Ho! Murder! Murder!
What may you be? Are you of good or evil?   65

Lodovico: As you shall prove us, praise us.

Iago: Signior Lodovico?

Lodovico: He, sir.

Iago: I cry you mercy. Here's Cassio hurt by villains.

Gratiano: Cassio?   70

Iago: How is it, brother?

Cassio: My leg is cut in two.

Iago: Marry, heaven forbid!
Light, gentlemen. I'll bind it with my shirt.

[*Enter Bianca.*]

Bianca: What is the matter, ho? Who is't that cried?

Iago: Who is't that cried?   75

Bianca: O my dear Cassio! My sweet Cassio!
O Cassio, Cassio, Cassio!

Iago: O notable strumpet! Cassio, may you suspect
Who they should be that thus have mangled you?

Cassio: No.   80

Gratiano: I am sorry to find you thus. I have been to seek you.

Iago: Lend me a garter. So. O for a chair
To bear him easily hence!

85	*trash:* referring to Bianca

94	*accidents:* events or unforeseen occurrences
95	*neglected:* ignored

98	*said:* done

100	*For:* as for
101	*Save you your labour:* Don't trouble yourself. Possibly meaning "leave him alone," or perhaps delivered sarcastically to suggest she is only acting upset. *He:* Roderigo

Bianca: Alas, he faints! O Cassio, Cassio, Cassio!

Iago: Gentlemen all, I do suspect this trash   85
 To be a party in this injury.
 Patience awhile, good Cassio. Come, come;
 Lend me a light. Know we this face or no?
 Alas, my friend and my dear countryman
 Roderigo? No. Yes, sure.—O heaven! Roderigo.   90

Gratiano: What, of Venice?

Iago: Even he, sir. Did you know him?

Gratiano: Know him? Ay.

Iago: Signior Gratiano? I cry you gentle pardon.
 These bloody accidents must excuse my manners
 That so neglected you.

Gratiano: I am glad to see you.   95

Iago: How do you, Cassio?—O, a chair, a chair!

Gratiano: Roderigo!

Iago: He, he, 'tis he! [*A chair brought in.*] O, that's well said; the chair.
 Some good man bear him carefully from hence.
 I'll fetch the general's surgeon. [*To Bianca.*] For you, mistress,   100
 Save you your labour. He that lies slain here, Cassio,
 Was my dear friend. What malice was between you?

Cassio: None in the world; nor do I know the man.

Iago: [*To Bianca.*] What, look you pale? O, bear him out o' the air.
                         [*Cassio and Roderigo are borne off.*]
 Stay you, good gentlemen. Look you pale, mistress?   105
 Do you perceive the gastness of her eye?
 Nay, if you stare, we shall hear more anon.
 Behold her well; I pray you, look upon her.
 Do you see, gentlemen? Nay, guiltiness will speak,
 Though tongues were out of use.   110

 [*Enter Emilia.*]

Emilia: 'Las, what's the matter? What's the matter, husband?

Iago: Cassio hath here been set on in the dark
 By Roderigo, and fellows that are 'scaped.
 He's almost slain, and Roderigo dead.

Emilia: Alas, good gentleman! Alas, good Cassio!   115

Iago: This is the fruit of whoring. Prithee, Emilia,

117   *know of:* find out from or ask

120   *charge:* order

122   *honest:* sexually honest or chaste

124   *see ... dress'd:* See that he gets his wounds tended to (dressed).
125   *tell's:* tell us

129   *fordoes:* destroys or ruins

Go know of Cassio where he supp'd to-night.
[*To Bianca.*] What, do you shake at that?
Bianca: He supp'd at my house; but I therefore shake not.
Iago: O, did he so? I charge you, go with me.   120
Emilia: Fie, fie upon thee, strumpet!
Bianca: I am no strumpet, but of life as honest
   As you that thus abuse me.
Emilia: As I? Foh? fie upon thee!
Iago: Kind gentlemen, let's go see poor Cassio dress'd.
   Come, mistress, you must tell's another tale.   125
   Emilia, run you to the citadel
   And tell my lord and lady what hath happ'd.   [*Exit Emilia.*]
   Will you go on? I pray.   [*Exeunt all but Iago.*]
               This is the night
   That either makes me or fordoes me quite.   [*Exit.*]

Act 5, Scene 1: Activities

1. Roderigo has evidently agreed to Iago's urging to kill Cassio so he can still pursue Desdemona. If you could step into his path and say something, anything, to Roderigo at this point, what would it be? How do you get through to people like that?

2. The opening of this scene sounds like an episode from a very bad TV murder mystery where the criminal attempts to cover his acts with murder. It never works.

   a) What makes Iago think that his plan will succeed? Are his reasons for the planned killings even sensible? One clue might be his comment about Cassio: "He hath a daily beauty in his life that makes me ugly." Is that a reason to kill somebody?

   OR

   b) With your experience as a modern-day detective, predict how you think Iago's whole scheme will turn out. Give your grounds for saying so. What prevents this episode from becoming farcical? Write a report for your investigation files, indicating your observations about this event. What might Iago tell you if you interviewed him as a witness?

3. Events move quickly in this scene and could be confusing for an audience. How would you, as a director, make certain that things remain clear to everybody, preventing the action from obscuring what is going on, especially in the fight scene? You will have to discuss with your actors your plans for choreographing all of the action to keep it obvious and understandable. Write your stage directions clearly so everybody in your cast knows exactly what is happening.

4. Up until now, Iago has just schemed but hasn't actually killed anybody. Why, all of a sudden, would he resort to murder? Is he desperate? Crazed? Clever? Imagine what is going on in Iago's mind at this time, and record it in your journal. Describe or draw the look on his face after the melee is over.

5. After all his manipulation of Cassio and his hatred for him, why does Iago immediately rush to Cassio's assistance? What does your group think? What do you think? Does he fool anybody? Does he fool himself? Why does he blame Bianca? If this is a strategy, what do you make of it? Decide in your group whether Iago is "thinking on his feet" or whether he staged this whole thing himself. Write a summary statement of your own in which you assess what went on here.

6. Why, all of a sudden, does everyone turn on Bianca? As her defence lawyer, what kind of defence could you prepare for her?

7. Iago says, "This is the night that either makes me or fordoes me quite." Decide with your group what he means by this statement. Does he know he might not succeed? Or does he feel truly confident? What do you think of Iago at this point — do you admire his courage and ingenuity, or are you appalled at what he is doing? Remember, although Roderigo is dead, Cassio is still alive. Share your ideas with the rest of the class.

For the next scene ...

Most serious, dramatic movies end with the death of someone you relate to very strongly. How do you feel about such endings? Do you think they are usually necessary to the story? Why or why not?

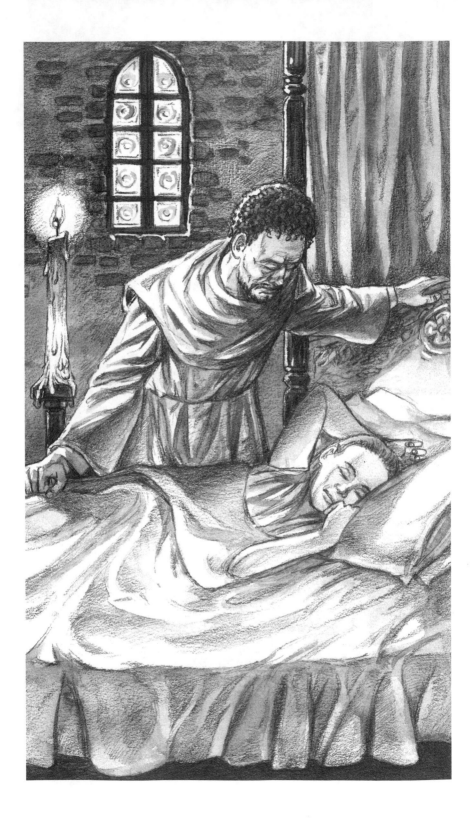

Act 5, Scene 2

In this scene ...

Desdemona lies asleep in her bed when Othello enters. He kisses her and, when she awakens, he gives her the opportunity to pray before she dies. In fear, she protests that she doesn't understand the talk of killing, so Othello accuses her of giving his handkerchief to Cassio. She denies this, telling him to simply ask Cassio for the truth. He tells her that Cassio admitted to his love for her before he died, so he cannot corroborate her innocence. Dismayed, she cries out. Othello smothers her. Emilia calls from outside the door to tell Othello about the melee in the streets and the murder. Othello thinks she is referring to Cassio. Just then Desdemona, not yet dead, cries out, protesting her innocence, and Othello confesses, "Twas I that kill'd her." He tells Emilia that Iago told him about Desdemona's infidelity. Emilia is stunned and shouts for help. The cries bring Gratiano, Montano, Iago, and others. Emilia accuses Iago of deception and Iago admits that he did inform against Desdemona. When Emilia reveals the truth about the handkerchief, Othello tries to kill Iago while Iago fatally stabs Emilia and flees. Montano and Gratiano run after Iago. Othello, now fully aware of what he has done, seizes a sword. When Iago is returned as a prisoner along with the wounded Cassio, Othello wounds Iago. He asks Cassio's forgiveness as the true story is revealed. Lodovico tells Othello he is to lose his command and Cassio will become governor of Cyprus. Othello is to be held prisoner to await trial. Protesting his great service to Venice, he stabs himself and falls dead on the bed next to Desdemona and Emilia. Iago is taken away to be tortured and executed.

1	*It is the cause:* Othello is perhaps reminding himself of Desdemona's "crime" as his justification for what he is about to do.
5	*monumental alabaster:* alabaster monuments (a translucent variety of gypsum used for fine sculptures or monuments)
6	*else:* otherwise
8	*flaming minister:* "flaming fire," as in a torch; "minister" means a servant
10	*Should I:* if I should; *but once:* but once I
11	*cunning'st:* most artfully created or skillfully made; *excelling:* superior to or surpassing
12	*Promethean heat:* divine fire. In mythology, Prometheus gave fire to humans.
13	*relume:* relight
17	*Justice ... sword:* The sword and scales were emblems of Justice; the scales weighed evidence, the sword punished.
20	*fatal:* deadly or destructive
21	*cruel tears:* tears that show no mercy or pity
26	*bethink yourself:* call to mind; *crime:* sin

Scene 2

*A bedchamber in the castle. Desdemona
in bed asleep; a light burning.
Enter Othello.*

Othello: It is the cause, it is the cause, my soul.
　Let me not name it to you, you chaste stars!
　It is the cause. Yet I'll not shed her blood,
　Nor scar that whiter skin of hers than snow,
　And smooth as monumental alabaster. 5
　Yet she must die, else she'll betray more men.
　Put out the light, and then put out the light.
　If I quench thee, thou flaming minister,
　I can again thy former light restore,
　Should I repent me; but once put out thy light, 10
　Thou cunning'st pattern of excelling nature,
　I know not where is that Promethean heat
　That can thy light relume. When I have pluck'd the rose,
　I cannot give it vital growth again;
　It needs must wither. I'll smell thee on the tree.　[*Kissing her.*] 15
　Ah, balmy breath, that dost almost persuade
　Justice to break her sword! One more, one more.
　Be thus when thou art dead, and I will kill thee,
　And love thee after. One more, and this the last.
　So sweet was ne'er so fatal. I must weep, 20
　But they are cruel tears. This sorrow's heavenly;
　It strikes where it doth love. She wakes.
Desdemona: Who's there? Othello?
Othello: 　　　　　　　　　　Ay, Desdemona.
Desdemona: Will you come to bed, my lord?
Othello: Have you pray'd to-night, Desdemon?
Desdemona: 　　　　　　　　　　　　　Ay, my lord. 25
Othello: If you bethink yourself of any crime

28   *Solicit for it straight:* pray for pardon immediately

29   *Alack:* alas

30   *walk by:* step aside

31   *I would not:* I do not wish to; *unprepared spirit:* kill her soul
by sending it to hell

32   *forfend:* forbid

37   *fatal:* deadly

45   *portents:* omens or signs of foreboding

46   *point on me:* predict my future; that is, they are not portents
for me

52   *presently:* immediately

54   *each article:* each item in the charge against you

Unreconciled as yet to heaven and grace,
  Solicit for it straight.
Desdemona: Alack, my lord, what may you mean by that?
Othello: Well, do it, and be brief; I will walk by.   30
  I would not kill thy unprepared spirit.
  No, heaven forfend! I would not kill thy soul.
Desdemona: Talk you of killing?
Othello: Ay, I do.
Desdemona: Then heaven
  Have mercy on me!
Othello: Amen, with all my heart!
Desdemona: If you say so, I hope you will not kill me.   35
Othello: Hum!
Desdemona: And yet I fear you; for you are fatal then
  When your eyes roll so. Why I should fear I know not,
  Since guiltiness I know not; but yet I feel I fear.
Othello: Think on thy sins.
Desdemona: They are loves I bear to you.   40
Othello: Ay, and for that thou diest.
Desdemona: That death's unnatural that kills for loving.
  Alas, why gnaw you so your nether lip?
  Some bloody passion shakes your very frame.
  These are portents; but yet I hope, I hope,   45
  They do not point on me.
Othello: Peace and be still!
Desdemona: I will so. What's the matter?
Othello: That handkerchief which I so loved and gave thee
  Thou gavest to Cassio.
Desdemona: No, by my life and soul!
  Send for the man and ask him.
Othello: Sweet soul, take heed,   50
  Take heed of perjury; thou art on thy death-bed.
Desdemona: Ay, but not yet to die.
Othello: Yes, presently.
  Therefore confess thee freely of thy sin;
  For to deny each article with oath
  Cannot remove nor choke the strong conception   55

56	*groan withal:* probably related to "conception" in that it suggests a woman in labour and perhaps expresses the overwhelming idea that has "given birth to" this drastic conception (belief), or Othello's desire to remove an unwanted child (Desdemona's supposed adultery)
59	*Offend:* sin against or wrong
60–61	*with ... love:* "Warranty" means authorization, so the reference is to the love that heaven authorizes us to feel for all human beings. *token:* a love token (the handkerchief)
62	*in's:* in his
63	*stone my heart:* harden my heart, like stone
68	*confess'd:* admitted to it
72	*ta'en order:* made arrangements or taken measures
75	*Had stomach:* would have had the appetite
76	*undone:* ruined or destroyed
82	*Being done:* The act will be done when the conflict between his love and honour is finished and his hand is ready to strike—there must be no hesitation once the decision is made or the act is begun.

That I do groan withal. Thou art to die.
Desdemona: Then Lord have mercy on me!
Othello: I say amen.
Desdemona: And have you mercy too! I never did
   Offend you in my life; never loved Cassio
   But with such general warranty of heaven   60
   As I might love. I never gave him token.
Othello: By heaven, I saw my handkerchief in's hand.
   O perjured woman! Thou dost stone my heart,
   And makest me call what I intend to do
   A murder, which I thought a sacrifice.   65
   I saw the handkerchief
Desdemona: He found it then.
   I never gave it him. Send for him hither.
   Let him confess a truth.
Othello: He hath confess'd.
Desdemona: What, my lord?
Othello: That he hath used thee.
Desdemona: How? unlawfully?
Othello: Ay.   70
Desdemona: He will not say so.
Othello: No, his mouth is stopp'd.
   Honest Iago hath ta'en order for't.
Desdemona: O, my fear interprets. What, is he dead?
Othello: Had all his hairs been lives, my great revenge
   Had stomach for them all.   75
Desdemona: Alas, he is betray'd, and I undone!
Othello: Out, strumpet! Weep'st thou for him to my face?
Desdemona: O, banish me, my lord, but kill me not!
Othello: Down, strumpet!
Desdemona: Kill me to-morrow; let me live to-night!   80
Othello: Nay, an you strive—
Desdemona: But half an hour!
Othello: Being done, there is no pause.
Desdemona: But while I say one prayer!
Othello: It is too late.
                            [*He smothers her.*]

84   Stage Direction: *Within*—offstage

91   *By and by:* soon
92   *'Tis like:* it is likely

94   *she:* Emilia
95   *she:* Desdemona

101   *yawn:* gape or open up, as in forming chasms; *alteration:* the change brought about by Desdemona's death

104   *Soft, by and by:* wait a moment; *curtains:* bed curtains

109   *error:* straying off course
110   *wont:* accustomed to
111   *mad:* from the Latin *"luna":* lunatic

Emilia: [*Within.*] My lord, my lord! What, ho, my lord, my lord!

Othello: What noise is this? Not dead? not yet quite dead?   85

    I that am cruel am yet merciful;

    I would not have thee linger in thy pain.

    So, so.

Emilia: [*Within.*] What, ho! my lord, my lord!

Othello: Who's there?

Emilia: [*Within.*] O, good my lord, I would speak a word with you! 90

Othello: Yes, 'tis Emilia. By and by. She's dead.

    'Tis like she comes to speak of Cassio's death.

    The noise was here. Ha! No more moving?

    Still as the grave. Shall she come in? Were't good?

    I think she stirs again. No. What's best to do?   95

    If she come in, she'll sure speak to my wife.

    My wife! My wife! What wife? I have no wife.

    O, insupportable! O heavy hour!

    Methinks it should be now a huge eclipse

    Of sun and moon, and that the affrighted globe   100

    Should yawn at alteration.

Emilia: [*Within.*]   I do beseech you

    That I may speak with you, O good my lord!

Othello: I had forgot thee. O, come in, Emilia.

    Soft, by and by. Let me the curtains draw.

    Where art thou?   [*Opens the door.*]

    [*Enter Emilia.*]   What's the matter with thee now?   105

Emilia: O my good lord, yonder's foul murder done!

Othello: What? Now?

Emilia: But now, my lord.

Othello: It is the very error of the moon.

    She comes more nearer earth than she was wont   110

    And makes men mad.

Emilia: Cassio, my lord, hath kill'd a young Venetian

    Called Roderigo.

Othello: Roderigo killed?

    And Cassio kill'd?

Emilia: No, Cassio is not kill'd.

Othello: Not Cassio kill'd? Then murder's out of tune,   115

119   *Out:* an expression of dismay

132   *folly:* unchastity
133   *belie:* tell lies about her
134   *false as water:* as unstable (false) as water

137–138 *I were ... grounds:* I would be damned to the deepest (lowest) level of hell if I had not had just reasons for my actions.

145   *chrysolite:* a semi-precious stone then thought to be the same as topaz. It is of a green colour.

And sweet revenge grows harsh.

Desdemona: O, falsely, falsely murder'd!

Emilia: Alas, what cry is that?

Othello: That? What?

Emilia: Out and alas! That was my lady's voice.
   Help! help, ho! help! O lady, speak again!   120
   Sweet Desdemona! O sweet mistress, speak!

Desdemona: A guiltless death I die.

Emilia: O, who hath done this deed?

Desdemona: Nobody; I myself. Farewell.
   Commend me to my kind lord. O, farewell!   [*Dies.*]   125

Othello: Why, how should she be murder'd?

Emilia: Alas, who knows?

Othello: You heard her say herself, it was not I.

Emilia: She said so. I must needs report the truth.

Othello: She's like a liar gone to burning hell.
   'Twas I that kill'd her.

Emilia: O, the more angel she,   130
   And you the blacker devil!

Othello: She turn'd to folly, and she was a whore,

Emilia: Thou dost belie her, and thou art a devil.

Othello: She was false as water.

Emilia: Thou art rash as fire to say
   That she was false. O, she was heavenly true!   135

Othello: Cassio did top her. Ask thy husband else.
   O, I were damn'd beneath all depth in hell
   But that I did proceed upon just grounds
   To this extremity. Thy husband knew it all.

Emilia: My husband?   140

Othello: Thy husband.

Emilia: That she was false to wedlock?

Othello: Ay, with Cassio. Nay, had she been true,
   If heaven would make me such another world
   Of one entire and perfect chrysolite,   145
   I'ld not have sold her for it.

Emilia: My husband?

Othello: Ay, 'twas he that told me first.

150   *iterance:* repetition
151   *made mocks with love:* made a mockery of love

155   *pernicious:* destructive, fatal

157   *bargain:* contract (marriage contract)

161   *Peace, you were best:* You had better be quiet.

163   *to be hurt:* to suffer hurt; *gull:* trick or dupe; *dolt:* simpleton
        or blockhead

177   *apt:* likely or credible

An honest man he is, and hates the slime
   That sticks on filthy deeds.
Emilia: My husband?
Othello: What needs this iterance, woman? I say thy husband.   150
Emilia: O mistress, villainy hath made mocks with love!
   My husband say that she was false?
Othello: He, woman.
   I say, thy husband. Dost understand the word?
   My friend, thy husband, honest, honest Iago.
Emilia: If he say so, may his pernicious soul   155
   Rot half a grain a day! He lies to the heart.
   She was too fond of her most filthy bargain.
Othello: Ha!
Emilia: Do thy worst.
   This deed of thine is no more worthy heaven   160
   Than thou wast worthy her.
Othello: Peace, you were best.
Emilia: Thou hast not half that power to do me harm
   As I have to be hurt. O gull! O dolt!
   As ignorant as dirt! Thou hast done a deed—
   I care not for thy sword; I'll make thee known,   165
   Though I lost twenty lives. Help! help! O, help!
   The Moor hath kill'd my mistress! Murder! murder!

[*Enter Montano, Gratiano, Iago, and others.*]

Montano: What is the matter? How now, general?
Emilia: O, are you come, Iago? You have done well,
   That men must lay their murders on your neck.   170
Gratiano: What is the matter?
Emilia: Disprove this villain, if thou be'st a man.
   He says thou told'st him that his wife was false.
   I know thou didst not; thou'rt not such a villain.
   Speak, for my heart is full.   175
Iago: I told him what I thought, and told no more
   Than what he found himself was apt and true.
Emilia: But did you ever tell him she was false?
Iago: I did.

183	*charm:* silence or still (as with a charm)
184	*bound:* duty bound
186	*forfend:* forbid
187	*set the murder on:* incited the murder
192	*then:* earlier, when she gave the handkerchief to Iago
194	*charge:* order
195	*leave:* permission
201	*uncle:* Gratiano, Desdemona's uncle and Brabantio's brother
203	*shows:* appears or seems
205	*match ... him:* Your marriage caused his death (was fatal to him).
206	*Shore ... twain:* cut in two his thread of life. In mythology, each person's life is controlled by the Three Fates. It is a thread spun by Clotho, measured out by Lachesis, and cut by Atropos. *Did he live:* if he had lived
207	*turn:* deed
208	*better angel:* guardian angel
209	*reprobation:* when a sinner is rejected by God. Gratiano feels that Othello's deed would have so devastated Desdemona's father that he would have taken his own life, which was considered to be a sin that led to damnation.
212	*A thousand times:* an indefinite number
213	*gratify:* reward

Emilia: You told a lie, an odious damned lie!   180
  Upon my soul, a lie, a wicked lie!
  She false with Cassio? Did you say with Cassio?
Iago: With Cassio, mistress. Go to, charm your tongue.
Emilia: I will not charm my tongue; I am bound to speak:
  My mistress here lies murder'd in her bed—   185
All: O heavens forfend!
Emilia: And your reports have set the murder on.
Othello: Nay, stare not, masters. It is true indeed.
Gratiano: 'Tis a strange truth.
Montano: O monstrous act!
Emilia: Villainy, villainy, villainy!   190
  I think upon't. I think I smell't—O villainy!
  I thought so then. I'll kill myself for grief.
  O villainy, villainy!
Iago: What, are you mad? I charge you get you home.
Emilia: Good gentlemen, let me have leave to speak.   195
  'Tis proper I obey him, but not now.
  Perchance, Iago, I will ne'er go home.
Othello: O! O! O!   [*He falls on the bed.*]
Emilia: Nay, lay thee down and roar!
  For thou hast kill'd the sweetest innocent
  That e'er did lift up eye.
Othello: [*Rising.*]   O, she was foul!   200
  I scarce did know you, uncle. There lies your niece,
  Whose breath, indeed, these hands have newly stopp'd.
  I know this act shows horrible and grim.
Gratiano: Poor Desdemona! I am glad thy father's dead.
  Thy match was mortal to him, and pure grief   205
  Shore his old thread in twain. Did he live now,
  This sight would make him do a desperate turn;
  Yea, curse his better angel from his side,
  And fall to reprobation.
Othello: 'Tis pitiful; but yet Iago knows   210
  That she with Cassio hath the act of shame
  A thousand times committed. Cassio confess'd it;
  And she did gratify his amorous works

214	*recognizance:* token

220	*liberal as the north:* as freely as the north wind blows (speaks)

223	Stage Direction: *offers*—tries

226	*fortune:* chance

233	*coxcomb:* literally, a fool's cap, therefore, a fool
234–235	*Are there ... thunder:* Has the thunder god, Jove, no stones left to use to strike down Iago, or does he need them all for thunder?

239	*notorious:* obvious or evident
240	*recover'd:* obtained
241	*without:* from the outside

With that recognizance and pledge of love
Which I first gave her. I saw it in his hand.   215
It was a handkerchief, an antique token
My father gave my mother.
Emilia: O heaven! O heavenly powers!
Iago: 'Zounds, hold your peace!
Emilia: 'Twill out, 'twill out! I peace?
No, I will speak as liberal as the north.   220
Let heaven and men and devils, let them all,
All, all, cry shame against me, yet I'll speak.
Iago: Be wise, and get you home.
Emilia: I will not.
                              [*Iago offers to stab Emilia.*]
Gratiano: Fie!
Your sword upon a woman!
Emilia: O thou dull Moor, that handkerchief thou speak'st of   225
I found by fortune, and did give my husband;
For often with a solemn earnestness,
More than indeed belong'd to such a trifle,
He begg'd of me to steal it.
Iago: Villainous whore!
Emilia: She give it Cassio? No, alas, I found it,   230
And I did give't my husband.
Iago: Filth, thou liest!
Emilia: By heaven, I do not, I do not, gentlemen.
O murderous coxcomb! What should such a fool
Do with so good a wife?
Othello: Are there no stones in heaven
But what serve for the thunder? Precious villain!   235
          [*He runs at Iago: Iago, from behind, stabs Emilia, and exit.*]
Gratiano: The woman falls. Sure he hath kill'd his wife.
Emilia: Ay, ay. O, lay me by my mistress' side.
Gratiano: He's gone, but his wife's kill'd.
Montano: 'Tis a notorious villain. Take you this weapon
Which I have here recover'd from the Moor.   240
Come, guard the door without. Let him not pass,
But kill him rather. I'll after that same villain,

244   *whipster:* literally, one who wields a whip, but here an insignificant or a contemptible person

245   *honour outlive honesty:* honourable reputation outlast honour itself

246   *bode:* predict

247   *I will play the swan:* an allusion to the belief that swans sang only once, just before death

253   *sword of Spain:* Toledo was famous for its swords. *the Ice-brook's temper:* Steel was tempered (strengthened) by plunging it red-hot into very cold water.

255   *dear:* dearly

258   *naked:* without weapon, unarmed

264   *your stop:* the obstruction you offer

267   *butt:* goal, limit, boundary

268   *sea-mark:* the boundary of the flow of the sea; perhaps also a beacon; *utmost sail:* farthest or last point; possibly his "final journey"

269   *go back:* move away from me; *lost:* groundless

270   *Man but a rush:* Use nothing more than a rush (bullrush) as a weapon.

273   *compt:* the day of reckoning (the Last Judgement)

For 'tis a damned slave.   [*Exeunt all but Othello and Emilia.*]
Othello: I am not valiant neither,
   But every puny whipster gets my sword.
   But why should honour outlive honesty?   245
   Let it go all.
Emilia: What did thy song bode, lady?
   Hark, canst thou hear me? I will play the swan,
   And die in music. [*Singing.*] *Willow, willow, willow.*
   Moor, she was chaste. She loved thee, cruel Moor:
   So come my soul to bliss as I speak true.   250
   So speaking as I think, I die, I die.   [*Dies.*]
Othello: I have another weapon in this chamber;
   It is a sword of Spain, the Ice-brook's temper.
   O, here it is. Uncle, I must come forth.
Gratiano: [*Within.*] If thou attempt it, it will cost thee dear.   255
   Thou hast no weapon, and perforce must suffer.
Othello: Look in upon me then and speak with me,
   Or, naked as I am, I will assault thee.

   [*Re-enter Gratiano.*]

Gratiano: What is the matter?
Othello: Behold, I have a weapon;
   A better never did itself sustain   260
   Upon a soldier's thigh. I have seen the day
   That with this little arm and this good sword
   I have made my way through more impediments
   Than twenty times your stop. But, O vain boast!
   Who can control his fate? 'Tis not so now.   265
   Be not afraid, though you do see me weapon'd.
   Here is my journey's end, here is my butt,
   And very sea-mark of my utmost sail.
   Do you go back dismay'd? 'Tis a lost fear.
   Man but a rush against Othello's breast,   270
   And he retires. Where should Othello go?
   Now, how dost thou look now? O ill-starr'd wench!
   Pale as thy smock! When we shall meet at compt,
   This look of thine will hurl my soul from heaven,

275–276   *Cold, cold, my girl ... chastity:* as chaste as ice and snow;
the opposite to the heat of lust

280   *steep-down gulfs:* pools bordered by steep cliffs

286   *I look down towards his feet:* to see whether they are cloven
like those of the devil

292   *in the practice of:* in the plotting or through the treachery of

295   *naught:* nothing

297   *consent in:* plan together or agree in planning

301   *demand:* ask; *demi-devil:* half-human and half-devil

305   *torments:* torture

And fiends will snatch at it. Cold, cold, my girl?   275
Even like thy chastity. O cursed slave!
Whip me, ye devils,
From the possession of this heavenly sight!
Blow me about in winds! roast me in sulphur!
Wash me in steep-down gulfs of liquid fire!   280
O Desdemona! Desdemona! dead!
Oh! Oh! Oh!

[*Enter Lodovico, Montano, Cassio carried in a chair, and Officers,
    with Iago, prisoner.*]

Lodovico: Where is this rash and most unfortunate man?
Othello: That's he that was Othello. Here I am.
Lodovico: Where is that viper? Bring the villain forth.   285
Othello: I look down towards his feet; but that's a fable.
   If that thou be'st a devil, I cannot kill thee.   [*Wounds Iago.*]
Lodovico: Wrench his sword from him.
Iago: I bleed, sir, but not kill'd.
Othello: I am not sorry neither. I'ld have thee live;
   For in my sense, 'tis happiness to die.   290
Lodovico: O thou Othello, that wert once so good,
   Fall'n in the practice of a damned slave,
   What shall be said to thee?
Othello: Why, anything:
   An honourable murderer, if you will;
   For naught did I hate, but all in honour.   295
Lodovico: This wretch hath part confess'd his villainy.
   Did you and he consent in Cassio's death?
Othello: Ay.
Cassio: Dear general, I never gave you cause.
Othello: I do believe it, and I ask your pardon.   300
   Will you, I pray, demand that demi-devil
   Why he hath thus ensnared my soul and body?
Iago: Demand me nothing. What you know, you know.
   From this time forth I never will speak word.
Lodovico: What, not to pray?
Gratiano: Torments will ope your lips.   305

307 *befall'n:* happened

310 *imports:* concerns

313 *gross:* flagrant, monstrous
314 *discontented paper:* letter filled with grievances and discontent

317 *belike:* probably

318 *caitiff:* villain

321 *but even:* just

323 *wrought to his desire:* worked out to his advantage or according to his plan

326 *Brave:* defy or challenge
327 *cast:* cast off, dismissed from office; *even but now he:* just now, Roderigo
329 *set him on:* incited him

332 *For:* as for

334 *hold him long:* keep him alive a long time
335 *close prisoner rest;* remain a closely guarded prisoner
336 *Till that:* until

338 *Soft you:* wait

Othello: Well, thou dost best.

Lodovico: Sir, you shall understand what hath befall'n,
 Which, as I think, you know not. Here is a letter
 Found in the pocket of the slain Roderigo,
 And here another. The one of them imports   310
 The death of Cassio to be undertook
 By Roderigo.

Othello: O villain!

Cassio: Most heathenish and most gross!

Lodovico: Now here's another discontented paper
 Found in his pocket too; and this, it seems,   315
 Roderigo meant to have sent this damned villain;
 But that, belike, Iago in the interim
 Came in and satisfied him.

Othello: O the pernicious caitiff!—
 How came you, Cassio, by that handkerchief
 That was my wife's?

Cassio: I found it in my chamber;   320
 And he himself confess'd but even now
 That there he dropp'd it for a special purpose
 Which wrought to his desire.

Othello: O fool! fool! fool!

Cassio: There is besides in Roderigo's letter,
 How he upbraids Iago that he made him   325
 Brave me upon the watch; whereon it came
 That I was cast; and even but now he spake
 After long seeming dead, Iago hurt him,
 Iago set him on.

Lodovico: You must forsake this room and go with us. 330
 Your power and your command is taken off,
 And Cassio rules in Cyprus. For this slave,
 If there be any cunning cruelty
 That can torment him much and hold him long,
 It shall be his. You shall close prisoner rest   335
 Till that the nature of your fault be known
 To the Venetian state. Come, bring away.

Othello: Soft you; a word or two before you go.

341	*unlucky:* unfortunate
343	*aught:* anything
345	*being wrought:* having been agitated or stirred up
346	*Perplex'd:* confused, puzzled, or perhaps distracted
347	*base Judean:* depraved Judean, possibly a reference to Judas Iscariot; *threw ... away:* betrayed or sacrificed Jesus
348	*Richer:* worth more; *subdued:* by grief
350–351	*Arabian trees ... gum:* probably myrrh trees, the gum of which is used for medicinal purposes
352	*Aleppo:* a significant staging post for trade between Europe and the East. It was said that the punishment there should a Christian strike a Turk was immediate death.
353	*malignant:* evil
354	*traduced the state:* insulted Venice and Venetians
357	*period:* ending, both of his speech and his life; *marr'd:* confused, unclear

361	*Spartan dog:* dogs of the Spartan breed were fierce and savage
362	*fell:* fierce and cruel
363	*loading:* load or burden
364	*object:* spectacle
365	*Let it be hid:* by drawing the curtains around the bed; *keep:* guard
367	*succeed on:* fall to, or are inherited by
368	*censure:* legal judgement and sentence
370	*straight aboard:* immediately depart (by ship)
371	*heavy:* sorrowful, distressing; *act:* deed or action

I have done the state some service, and they know't.
No more of that. I pray you, in your letters, 340
When you shall these unlucky deeds relate,
Speak of me as I am. Nothing extenuate,
Nor set down aught in malice. Then must you speak
Of one that loved not wisely, but too well;
Of one not easily jealous, but, being wrought, 345
Perplex'd in the extreme; of one whose hand,
Like the base Judean, threw a pearl away
Richer than all his tribe; of one whose subdued eyes,
Albeit unused to the melting mood,
Drop tears as fast as the Arabian trees 350
Their medicinal gum. Set you down this;
And say besides that in Aleppo once,
Where a malignant and a turban'd Turk
Beat a Venetian and traduced the state,
I took by the throat the circumcised dog 355
And smote him, thus.   [*Stabs himself.*]
Lodovico: O bloody period!
Gratiano: All that's spoke is marr'd.
Othello: I kiss'd thee ere I kill'd thee. No way but this,
   Killing myself, to die upon a kiss.   [*Falls on the bed and dies.*]
Cassio: This did I fear, but thought he had no weapon; 360
   For he was great of heart.
Lodovico: [*To Iago.*]   O Spartan dog,
   More fell than anguish, hunger, or the sea!
   Look on the tragic loading of this bed.
   This is thy work. The object poisons sight;
   Let it be hid. Gratiano, keep the house, 365
   And seize upon the fortunes of the Moor,
   For they succeed on you. To you, lord governor,
   Remains the censure of this hellish villain,
   The time, the place, the torture. O, enforce it!
   Myself will straight aboard, and to the state 370
   This heavy act with heavy heart relate.   [*Exeunt.*]

Act 5, Scene 2: Activities

1. When Othello enters the bedroom, it appears that Desdemona is sleeping. How, then, would he deliver his first speech so she doesn't hear it and waken? What does he say of significance in this speech that he hasn't already said? Is he filled with emotion as he speaks, or is he calculating and rational? Decide what you think, and then exchange your views with others. Might this speech be delivered as a soliloquy? Does it change your perception of Othello in any way? In your production, would you have Othello kiss Desdemona? What would be the difference if you didn't? When you have resolved these issues, write an account of how this scene should be portrayed on stage, or, if you envision a movie version, what would be your focus?

2. Oddly, Othello offers Desdemona the opportunity to pray before she dies. To many this is macabre, horrific, and cold. Why would he do this? With your group, discuss this "strangling" scene. Most regard it as appalling and unconscionable, yet Othello feels the murder is justified. How would Othello possibly argue that he was justified in strangling his wife? Write the confession he might make after his arrest.

3. Shakespeare's plays do not often show violent scenes such as this one on stage. Why do you suppose he felt it necessary to do so in this play? Share your views with others in the class, and write your own opinion about the validity of stage violence of this sort. If you were a film censor, how would you justify its inclusion?

4. Emilia's talk of murder simply underscores Desdemona's final protestations of innocence and her inexplicable defence of Othello, who doesn't believe any of it. How would you have him utter the words, "'Twas I that killed her."? What kind of man is this, anyway? If you were a juror hearing Othello's explanation of why he has committed murder, would you be sympathetic to him? If you weren't, what penalty would you recommend?

5. For some reason, Emilia is also killed by Iago. Is he now out of control and truly crazed? What possible defence could you muster for this man? What would you do as Gratiano? How would you explain any of this to people who weren't there? As a reporter, interview Gratiano and find out what he has to say.

6. How is it possible that Othello suddenly wakes up and realizes what he has done, only to stick by his notion that he did what he did to protect his honour. How important is honour to you? Could you possibly have done what Othello did? Many gangs believe that honour is what sets them apart and keeps them a "family." What are your views on that notion of honour? In your journal, define what you think "honour" means, and decide how far you would go to defend it. Decide how much honour cost Othello, and consider what good it does to go to such great lengths to defend it.

7. Lodovico, who seems an insignificant figure at the beginning of the play, has the last word. What do you think is his understanding of what happened in Cyprus? Do you agree with him? Are you uplifted by this dramatic experience or are you depressed by it?

8. As in a murder mystery, all is explained by Roderigo's letters. This is clearly a dramatic device to end the play. While it is a convention, is it acceptable and satisfying? Are you pleased that Cassio is still alive to live his "happily ever after" story? As Cassio, would you forgive Othello? Is forgiveness the "message" of the play? If not, what is this play about, in your view? As you discuss this with your group or with the class, you might also consider what impact the play has had on you and comment about that in your final journal entry.

Act 5: Consider the Whole Play

1. The politics in this play are kept largely in the background, but nevertheless they are there. What do you think is going on in Venice while events are focused in Cyprus? How long would it take to get from Venice to Cyprus in 1600? How long would it take for relevant news to arrive from one place to the other? In reality, could the events in this play possibly have happened in the period of time suggested in the play itself? How important, then, is time in a play?

2. When things go horribly wrong, people want to assign blame to somebody or something. Who gets the blame for what went wrong in Cyprus?

3. Create a cartoon strip illustrating a significant plot point from the play.

4. Create a commercial for a made-for-TV version of *Othello* as a kind of infomercial focusing on the benefits of watching this play. What highlights would you show without giving the whole thing away? What is your central selling point?

5. Create a rap version of this play in 100 lines or less.

6. You are a guest on a TV talk show. The topic is "great Shakespearean plays." You have chosen *Othello* as your play of choice. What do you say about it that might keep a daytime audience—used to family disputes, mangled marriages, abusive husbands, and difficult children—interested in what you are saying?

7. Create a photo essay that would capture the essence of this play. You might want to do this by recording contemporary faces, landscapes, signs, and neighbourhoods, and juxtaposing the images so you get the effect you want. You could turn this into a visual presentation complete with music to reinforce the mood you are trying to create.

8. Stage a press conference in which you discuss the final tragic events of the play for a live television news report from the castle in Cyprus. Invite questions from the townspeople

(the class), but be prepared for some tough ones. Do you answer them all?

9. Gather Iago, Cassio, Othello, Roderigo, Desdemona, Emilia, and Bianca together at a dinner party. Have them discuss their problems and focus on the fact that each has felt misunderstood. In a group, choose one character each and re-enact this discussion for your classmates.

10. Put Shakespeare on trial for having created such a dismal picture of humanity. You might want to set this up as a real trial with a prosecutor and a defence counsel and with witnesses for both sides. The judge will make the final decision as to whether or not Shakespeare is guilty of misrepresenting human beings in general.

11. You have decided to keep an account of the most memorable lines from this play to put in your Dictionary of Great Sayings. Which ones will you select?

12. If you could talk to anybody from this play, who would it be and why? What would you say to this person to open the conversation?

13. Some people think this is a multicultural play that addresses issues relating to different races and cultures. In fact, one director said that he was convinced it was about race. What is your response to that? Do all actors who play Othello have to be black to make the play authentic? Doesn't Othello engineer his own demise? Couldn't anybody do that?

14. If you wanted to update this play or perform it as a contemporary musical, how would you do it? You would have to change the dialogue into contemporary language, recreate the setting, and redefine the characters without losing any of the sense of the original text. Create an outline of how you might accomplish this.

15. If jealousy could have a character and a persona, what would it look like? (Iago calls it "the green-eyed monster" in Act 3, but that is only his point of view at the time.) Create your own picture concept, and then write a magazine article as an interview with this "being" you have created.

16. While the play was originally performed during the day, what sort of lighting would you use, as a director, to reinforce the mood of each act? Pay careful attention to internal evidence to support your choices.